Effects of
Social Media Advertisement
on Buying Behaviour

Dr. Supriya Pathak

Woven Words Publishers Pvt. Ltd.

Registered Office:
Vill: Raipur, P.O: Raipur Paschimbar, Dist: Purba Midnapore, Pin: 721401, West Bengal, India.

www.wovenwordspublishers.com
Email: wovenwordspublishers@gmail.com

First published by Woven Words Publishers Pvt. Ltd., 2019

Copyright© Dr. Supriya Pathak, 2019

Branch Office(Operational): Hyderabad-500008

IMPRINT: WOVEN WORDS ACADEMIC

RESEARCH WORK

ISBN 13: 978-93-86897-95-4
ISBN 10: 93-86897-95-4

Price: $ 15 USD/ ₹ 300 INR

Printed and bound in India

ACKNOWLEDGEMENT

Completion of this doctoral dissertation was possible with the support of several people. I would like to express my sincere gratitude to all of them. First of all, I am extremely grateful to my research guide, **Prof. (Dr.) Unmesh Mandloi**, for his valuable guidance, scholarly inputs and consistent encouragement I received throughout the research work.

I am thankful to **Prof. (Dr.). Rajendra Jain, Dean (FMS & Research),** for the academic support and the facilities provided to carry out the research work at the Institute. His guidance helped me in all the time of research and writing of this thesis.

I express my special regards to **Dr. K.L Thakral (Chancellor), Dr. Devendra Pathak (Vice Chancellor), Dr. Dhruv Ghai (Pro Vice Chancellor), Dr. Gaima Ghai (Dean Achedemics), Mr. Lalit Awasthi (Registrar), Mr. Kumar Pragulbh (Assistant Registrar), Oriental** University Indore forever helping support during the course of research work.

No research is possible without the Library, the Centre of learning resources. I take this time to express my gratitude to all the library staff for their services.

I am thankful to **Mr. Rahul Supeakar, (Wipro Technologies**) and **Mr. Alok Upadhyay (IBM Global Services)** for wonderful support in collecting data from IT companies.

I am grateful to my husband **Prof. (Dr.) Ravindra Pathak,** who has provided me through moral and emotional support in my life. I am also grateful to my other family members and one of my friends **Mr. Ashish Kushwah** and all who have supported me along the way.

I am very much indebted to my family specially my parents Shri Jagadish Chandra Tiwari, and Smt Krishana Tiwai, my sister Ms. Anjali Tiwari, My in laws Shri Madanlal Pathak and Smt Kamlesh Pathak and my two kids Diya and Kalki who supported me in every possible way for the completion of this work. In addition, I also want to show my gratitude towards my life coach Advocate Santosh Sukla ji who helped me through his life lessons.

Above all, I owe it all to Almighty God for granting me the wisdom, health and strength to undertake this research task and enabling me to its completion.

EFFECT OF SOCIAL MEDIA ADVERTISEMENT ON BUYING BEHAVIOUR

ABSTRACT

Social media has created a huge buzz in today's world. It is very popular in the millennial generations, but the middle and the older generations are also not untouched by the wave of social media. On domestic front it is used for interacting with friends and relatives and for the purpose of socializing. On professional front, it has been widely used for acquiring markets by new business ventures. Many established organizations are undergoing operational change in their traditional practices in order to adapt to this online environment for promoting their products and services globally.

Social media has been the most recent and booming technological innovations. It offers a wide range of benefits. Interest and curiosity to gain more knowledge in the field of social media has been the main ground for selecting the topic of Social media for the research purpose. Also much research has not been done on social media in the Indian context and more precisely in Information Technology Processionals; therefore Social Media has been selected as the topic for research.

As stated above, the study sought to find out the impact of social media advertisements buying behaviour of millennial it professionals for electronic gadgets. Study objectives were formulated and research questions were derived from the objectives. Questionnaires were the instruments used in collection of data. Quantitative data collected, was then coded and inputted in statistical package for social science (SPSS).

The study has been conducted in two phases. Initially in Phase-I, Exploratory research has been conducted. For the same purpose formal interactions were conducted with those millennial working IT professional, who use online sites for buying consumer electronics products. After the interactions, the variables of the study had been identified and accordingly the questionnaire was prepared. In Phase-II, a Descriptive study had been conducted. The secondary data had been collected from various available resources.

Review of Literature from various published reports, research journals, reference books and online databases.

The data collected from questionnaire were scored and tabulated into a master data sheet. The data was analyzed with the help of statistical package SPSS 17. The mean scores arrived are put to various statistical analysis using various statistical tools in order to test the research hypothesis. The statistical tools applied included Chi-Square test, Regression, Anova, Rank Order Co-efficient etc.

In view of the result of research work evident that social media played a major role on behavior change of the respondents. The millennial mostly used social media for purchasing the electronics gadget and social media platform influencing the buying behaviour in different ways. The fact that social media is part of them especially having been born in this era of emerging technology, most felt that they could not do without it.

From the study it has been concluded that Face book is the most preferred Social networking site that targets the advertisements to specific group of audience according to the young millennial. Face book is followed by LinkedIn and the least preferred site for targeting the advertisements to specific group of audience is Twitter. By the analysis of study also revealed that several drivers, motives and reasons affect the buying behavior of the millennial like Personnel Involvement level, available online price, spending time on social media network, frequency of visit advertisement, brand, brand reputation, price comparison with other brand, product attribute, product quality, function ability, value, worth and previous relationship and experience with brand.

Since the study targeted on the general social media, a study can be done further on the specific social media platform, such as Facebook or Twitter. While the study recognized that social media has impacts on other age groups outside the youth bracket.

Keywords: Social Media, Social Media Advertisement, Millennial, Buying Behaviour

PREFACE

The emergence of Internet and social media is one of the most formidable developments in the history of marketing and advertisements. Social media is an evolution based on the internet, where not only it encourages user generated contents, but also extends the focus to the users by allowing them to exhibit contents to share among networks. This particular technical revolution during the last decade has drastically revolutionized the traditional marketing approaches and brought marketers to a new era. In the new marketing era, the social media advertisements has likely to revolutionize the relationships marketers have with retailers, channels of distribution, their ultimate consumers, etc. It is an Information Age, and consumers are inundated with overwhelming quantities of information each and every day, whereas millennial are a technologically sophisticated generation, who has the purchasing power to change the face of retailing. A significant proportion of their shopping is done online and they utilize their social networks while engaging in the shopping process.

Millennial have embraced social media and use it to gain and share information about companies/brands through reviews, ratings, videos and other referrals. This idea of using social influence and word of mouth through social media is changing the way commerce functions. It is important that businesses attempt to understand and target this generation of tech-savvy, connected, multi-channel shoppers. These millennial are shaping the future and social influenced purchases are poised to explode over the next several years.

Consumer electronics was the first segment, which started the online marketing for sale and motivated another segment for increase the presence in the field of digital online marketing. This segment invented the marketing strategy based on online user and study the feedback of customer for increasing the quality and reduction in cost with the customize view of product. Consumer electronics area using very effectively videos of the products on the social networking sites, which is very useful and understandable by the customer and it is necessary for customer satisfaction and increasing the sale by online social media platforms.

Most studies show that the Internet and social media usage is changing consumer behavioral modern trend also witnessed in India. This research work offer an overview on how the consumers specially millennial use social media and social media advertisements in the stages of decision making process and the psychographic variables that influence their consumer behavior. A survey of information technology professional millennial selected randomly in the Indore was conducted, to find out to what extent they are impacted by the use of social media, and what role it plays in their decision making process. Social media has gained a lot of popularity over the past few years and as a result of this popularity, other traditional Media have experienced decline in both business and popularity. Now the main stream media channels have faced many challenges in recent times that have led to closure with TV facing down turn in their profits levels. As a result of completion and tough economic environment, companies have tightened their budgets especially advertising budgets which have shifted to online channels.

The entire purpose of this research is to consider and analyze the effect of social media advertisement on social networking sites like Facebook, twitter on customer behavior. Now in the technological edge social media is powerful tool and influencing the customer behavior and shaping the perception about product and services.

The motive of the research was triggered by personal interest in how consumer behavior has changed in the digital age, in particular with social media advertisement. The amount of information available to us increases in each new day; as a result, we are overwhelmingly exposed and attained to different aspects of information via the Social Web. The accessibility and transparency that social media offers has led changes in how consumers position themselves in today's market, in which it is inevitable and necessary for companies to equip with a new marketing mindset.

The central gravity of the research was to explain why, when, and how social media advertisements has impacted on consumer decision making process both in theory and in practice. The research was carried out in the perception of consumers (for electronics products), which was aimed to explain the impacts of social media advertisements on different stages in their decision making process, by finding out how consumers perceive social media advertisements in the entire process.

CONTENTS

LIST OF TABELS

5.32	Millennial who not consider any given attribute.	78
5.33	Millennial who visit shop before final decision of purchasing product	79
5.34	Relationship between consumer buying behaviour with the appealing factor of social media advertisement towards advertisements displayed on SNS .	80
5.35	Symmetric Measures to determine how much relationship exists in between consumer buying behaviour and the appealing factor of social media advertising towards advertisements displayed on SNS	81
5.36	Relationship between consumer buying behaviour with the factor of memorable visuals and slogans of the advertisements displayed on SNS	82
5.37	Relationship between consumer buying behaviour with the attractive factor of the advertisements displayed on SNS .	83
5.38	Relationship between consumer buying behaviour with the trustworthiness factor of the advertisements displayed on SNS .	85
5.39	Relationship between online purchase behaviour with the appealing factor of social media advertisements displayed on SNS	86
5.40	Relationship between online purchase behaviour with the factor of social media advertising i.e. memorable visuals and slogans of the advertisements displayed on SNS .	87
5.41	Relationship between online purchase behaviour with the trust factor of social media advertising	90
5.42	Relationship between complex buying behaviour with the appealing factor of social media advertising	91
5.43	Relationship between complex buying behaviour with the memorable visuals and slogans factor of social media advertising	92

5.106	Interested to provide online customer rating of telephone instruments	133
5.107	Interested to provide online customer rating of mobile phones	133
5.108	Interested to provide online customer rating of videogames	136
5.109	Interested to provide online customer rating of Camcorders	136
5.110	Frequency of millennial who study customer reviews before purchasing	138
5.111	Frequency of millennial who study customer reviews before purchasing	138

LIST OF FIGURES

ABBREVIATIONS

SNS:	Social Networking Sites.
SM:	Social Media.
IMC:	Integrated Marketing Communications.
CRM:	Customer Relationship Management.
FMCG:	Fast Moving Consumer Goods.
PR:	Public Relations
EWOM:	Electronic Word of Mouth
PCAP:	Perceived Community Attitude Toward a Product
SERP:	Search Engine Ranking Position
CPC:	Cost per Click
USD:	US Dollar
MNC:	Multi-National Company

Chapter 1

Introduction

In the new age of technological advancement and competition, every business needs specific and competitive marketing strategies for retain market share and increase profit of business. In present time the most promising and technical marketing strategy that can be used for specific customers or group of people without any more investment is the use of social media as a marketing tool for your specified customers.

Basically social media has been internet based innovation for creating and maintaining social network but now days that converted into groups of people and by the help of marketing tool, it can be converting into the group of specific customer.

In the 21st century, everything depends on the internet and daily life is fully dependent on the availability of internet and social media platform creating an online circle of family and friends, so in the next few decades business, social network will be a big internet hub of all purchasing and related activity. With the spreading of this new technology millennial playing very crucial role because they know about technology and its application in everyday life. This is the new edge of online relation and online purchasing with more reliable and efficient way without consuming time.

This is time of information technology era and basis of all innovation and technological advancement, so that is the main reason for selecting the area related with social media advertisement with emphasis of millennial especially for the information technology Professional and added absolutely in Indore, which is the next hub of information technology development. Now technology is spreading from metro cities to non-metro and rural areas and for marketing strategies that is necessary to analysis the effect of social media in these areas.

1.1 Social Media

Jim Ellis and Tom Truscott in 1979 created a platform on which the user can communicate through the messages without restriction of physical boundaries and that was the basis of social media and internet. After that Bruce and Susan founded the first generation social networking website for combining all online writers into one platform called "Weblog" and now it is converted into blog.

With the growth of internet, social media sites like My Space, Orkut and face book also started and new term " social media" started with initial objective of social connectivity with friends and family beyond physical boundary around the world.

Social Media basically internet based accumulation social networking platform, it accepts content generated by any person which is associated with the platform which can be social message or customer feedback of any content .The social media is basically advanced version of a web 2.0 internet enabled platform, which can be share the ideas and express the communication without physical boundaries around the world.

Now in the time of globalization, the main requirement of companies and production house is development and implementation of technological upgraded marketing strategies which can increase the sell and profit of the company. In the time of internet the most promising new technology in marketing is use of social media. Internet based Social media now acutely activating and game changer tool in the new era of marketing and competition. It has accepted that social media, to be acutely advantageous tools which can be efficiently manage and add groups of people and community for the business purpose.

In the field of internet based marketing tool social media has been the lot of contempt and innovative invention of 21st century. It offers an advanced field of benefits for marketing. Interest and concern to accretion added ability is the main reason for the investing this topic. Plentiful analysis not done in the area of social media marketing especially for the millennial information technology Professional and in Indore, which is the next hub of information technology development.

1.2   User of Social Media

Social media and its use in advertising is very new field and continuously growing with the growth of internet and awareness of people, so this area is very emerging and interesting and that is the main reason for selecting the topic for research.

With the growth of internet rational acceleration started in the users of internet for using the social networking sites. In last few years (from 2007) around 60% of internet user acclimated the SNS platform on different websites. At this time the advancement of social media not limited only up to the millennial but also spreading in the matured aged people in the form of beginners, bloggers and social content writers.

The growth of social media user in 2008 crossed the capital Social platforms beyond the apple a part of 17, 0000 internet surfers. The content available in the different blogs and accounts also increased from 64% to 78% in couple of years. The bloggers and content writers also increased from 30 to 45 % whereas user based SNS platform for video sharing also increased up to 85% in few years of launching the SNS websites. The growth of social media is the history in the spreading of technology based innovation.

China, South Korea, India like Asian countries has the highest internet users and accordingly they are participating in the adding of the content in the social platforms. In Latin America also the user increasing very rapidly. At the starting time of SNS, in United States and Europe the acceptance level was low but now they are also participating very rapidly in all platforms of social media.

1.3   Advertisements

In the modern world, our product and service consumption habits completely dependent on the advertisement on the different mediums. In the marketing field also, they accept as well become a basic aspect of the advertising world and lots of money is getting assigned by companies appear their advertisement budget in this area. In last few years advertisement has acquired to an abundant admeasurements. At the time of technological advancement lots of options available for advertisement according to the requirement of target group and financial availability.

Followings are different types of advertisements, using according to the specific purpose and availability of resources.

Print media is very conventional and old method of advertisements in which advertisements print on the newspaper, magazine, booklets and circulate in the groups of people.

Guerrilla Advertisement is a basically unconventional method of advertisements, in which allow to customer for the actively participation with the creative ideas of advertisers. It spreads normally mouth to mouth publicity and discussion on different platforms like social media.

Broadcast advertisement is a mass advertising methods, in which through the television and radio advertisement can be spread in groups of people.

Outdoor advertisement basically covers the area outside of home by boxboard, road show, and banner.

Public service advertisement used by the government or Nongovernmental organizations for the educating about public health, rules not for commercial purpose.

Product promotion advertisement used for the promotion or launching of new products and it is associated with lots of advertisement activities related with quality and feature aspect of the product.

Mobile advertisement is the new way of advertisements and it is spreading with the social networking platform like face book, twitter .Normally this applications used in smart phones and it is very rapidly growing method of advertisements.

Online advertisement is the new technological advance internet based method of advertisements, in which advertisement spreads through the different websites related with product, search engines like Google, yahoo , promotional E- mail, advertisements on different social networking platforms, banner on different chat websites. It is economical and very effective approach for targeting of specific group or community of people.

1.4 Buying Behaviour

Buying behavior is basically group of activities of the person at the time of purchasing, using and consuming the product or services. Consumer behavior is basically integration of product or service information, approach or method, opinion and activities of involved person.

Customer purchasing behavior is basically a study of customer behavior at the time of purchasing or time of gathering the information about product. Customer behavior is a long term study about the way of customer to analysis the product, market survey and research for the particular product. In this study also involved about factors affecting the customer purchasing decision and what are the changes come at the time of purchasing of different type of product.

1.5 Types of Buying Behaviour

When the customer purchase very expensive products like laptop, this time customer shows fully involvement in the product, this is called complex behavior. If the customer using the products from very long time and very aware about the quality and prices of different brands like bread, this type of behavior called habitual behavior.

At the time of expensive product purchasing, if different brands available at the same or very little price difference. This time customer behavior changed from complex behavior and it is known as dissonance reducing behavior. In the variety seeking behavior, if different brands available of the same product like cooking oil, this time customer change the brands only for satisfaction or wants to use another brand and if the customer visit any shop and can't resist to purchase the product like cloth& watches , this type of behavior called impulsive buying behavior.

Online Buying Behaviour:

In present research work more emphasis on the impact of social network advertisements on the online buying behavior of the customer. Use of new method of technological marketing changing human behaviour for purchasing the product or services. The emergence of social media networking created a lot of challenges to the marketing policy maker of companies for retain profit and increasing sales through the SNS platform.

The major aspects of consumer behaviour including gathering product information, product research, customer's online feedback, reviews, post purchase opinion affected by social media network.

Basically social media users afraid to analysis of related information on net. Customers want useful information in short format of product or service about quality, appearance. So normally online consumers use timesaving methods available on social networking sites like banner, product gallery, customer reviews.

Online user normally prefers customer reviews not suggestions from websites. Online information influencing the consumer behavior of customer products including vacation and outside dinner also. Response of customer views on the advertisements and the websites is very important, for effective advertisements and satisfaction of the online customers.

Ability of understanding customer behavior is very important for effective marketing policy. It is very difficult to understand the behavior of the customer because customer can be influence on good customer review only and sometime costly advertisements cannot influence the customer.

Secondly, customer can change their decision at any time due to different reasons so customer behavior prediction is very difficult because of different parameter and factor related with buying behavior. So accurate knowledge about the customer is very relevant for an good marketing strategy

Concept of Advertising on Social Networking sites:

Basically the SNS is the social networking platform like face book, but now it's converted into the business platform, can be use by giving advertisement on the websites. Business promotion now possible with the payment for advertisement on social networking sites for the concern community or the group of peoples. These types of advertisement are more effective and play a better role in advertisement communication and for specific group of peoples.

1.6   Social Media Advertisements

Marketing strategy on SNS platform affected by current trends of internet in world. Due to the high costs incurred associated for advertisement of mass peoples, advertisers are searching other ways of conventional advertisements and finding the new way of advertisements in social media networks through paid advertisements for target group of customers.

The emerging area of unconventional way of advertisements like SNS platform helped companies as compared to the other available mediums in different parameters like very systematic, targeted and appropriate acquaintance. So now the social media advertisements is not only useful for large and big companies as well as it is very useful for new entrepreneurs, SME ventures and even NGO and different governmental organizations..

This time print and television medium is very costly for marketing as compare to marketing over the social media. Now companies communicating with consumers through a online, articulate SNS platforms like face book, twitter, LinkedIn and other sites for sharing the audio, video and different available online platforms.

With the help of SNS only, customers are very active in the field of customer feedback, online rating and different blogs. This time customers also visiting different websites for analysis and collecting the product information and by the like and support of the customer only SNS platform marketing can be success.

Now by the different reasons customer not interested in the conventional sources of advertisements like print and promotional and with the help of Social Media searching the product information and taking buying decision.

Therefore anticipate that advertisements on social media a basic factor of the company marketing strategy. This is an important factor to acquaint with their targeted market. Marketing on the internet based social networking sites in ten times more effective than other means of marketing.

Basic and fundamental reason for using advertisements on social media because on the online market targeting of particular community and age group is very easy, in conventional marketing that is not possible.

Secondly, Advertisements on SNS accustomed freedom to the producer and buyer, which was not available before. Most important thing is companies have no power to change, continuance and abundance, which is the part of communication on SNS about the product.

The concurrence in the middle of business and customer is variation with the addition of SNS. Social media influence the buying behavior of customer in different aspects. After the emergence of social media networking, only good customer relationship is the basis of business and growth in the age of online marketing.

In a report of social media networking sites, face book had a more effective way to influence buying behavior of customer rather than twitter and other SNS websites. Now a day's lots of product information, customer reviews are available on the different platform and customers are educating each other about product quality, service policy, and company behavior etc. the presence of big market leaders on face book and other networking sites not only for increasing the sales but they also wants to change the conventional process of purchasing for cost minimization.

At the time of launching the Vivo laptop by Sony Company, the whole advertisements strategy was based on the marketing on social media advertisements on face book and twitter. This time company given the discounted price on the social media advertisements on twitter and sale increased by 1.5 million USD. The main objective was Sony company about the awareness of the consumer and increase the sales by customize and target based advertisements between the youngster and consumer.

In another case study of IBM Company, increased the sales by simply following and understand the customer voice on the social media network. Consumer electronics company dell also increased its profit by social media networking.

This is very surprising but customer behavior about the purchasing through social media are rapidly changing, In comparison of normal internet user, face book and twitter user are engaging in more purchasing through online platform. This websites creating trust about the product and service and boosting the customer confidence.

1.7 IT Professionals and Social Networking

 IT professionals creating active driving force for effectiveness with growth for the social networking and mostly IT professionals use the social networking platform. In social networking sites major users are millennial and they know about technological developments and its use in daily life.

Basically social networking sites are connecting old friends, making new friends online around the world without physical boundaries and that is possible only in the development of information technology.

 IT professionals are application SNSs to connect with their old friends, making new ones, as maintain advance Social ties with their circle across the world.

1.8 Consumer Electronics Segment and Social Media

Consumer electronics was the first segment, which started the online marketing for sale and motivated another segment for increase the presence in the field of digital online marketing. This segment invented the marketing strategy based on online user and study the feedback of customer for increasing the quality and reduction in cost with the customize view of product.

New online marketing advertisement adopted by consumer electronic items manufacturer and now also using application and rather emphasizing on the online customers more compared to other manufacturers.

The antagonism in the term of price, brand and customer comfort , now the companies are going in the field of online marketing because social media is an acute weapon in this competitive edge.

In the field of consumer electronics, Philips was the first company launched the customer friendly website in 2007, for new change in the satisfactory product approach for the consumers acquainted the new experience . Philips got a big deal due to online marketing and sold 70 million products.

In the study that is proved that social media is very good method of advertisements for the companies because on this platform we can give the answer of customer questions, whereas in the traditional platform companies can provide one sided information and cannot solve the customer quires.

In the reports of GK Technologies has apparent about the nine points increased in the Customer Confidence basis for digital media. That's why most of the companies concentrating about digital media advertisements.

Sony launched the social media platform in 2005 for the launching of its new product bravia LCD Television and the success of this social media advertisement was the eye opener for the rest market and only after this success main player of consumer electronics started the presence on the social media network.

Launching of new LED television by Toshiba on the social media network platform and its success and customer feedback was excellent.

At the time of launching new digital camera ZX , Panasonic company also started the presence on the social media network and got the good success in the sales promotion,

Online feedback and customer comments very important for the promotion of products on the social media platform. On this platform only customer can ask the questions and can solve the queries.

Consumer electronics area using very effectively videos of the products on the social networking sites, which is very useful and understandable by the customer and it is necessary for customer satisfaction and increasing the sale by online social media platforms.

The growth in online review, customer feedback is sign for shifting the trends in marketing strategies. Now digital marketing and advertisement on social network is very essential not only for increasing the sales as well as increment in the customer satisfaction and awareness about the product and technical support to the customer. Television, music player, video recorder etc. considered for the research as a consumer electronics product.

Chapter 2

Literature Review

The entire purpose of this research is to consider and analyze the effect of social media advertisement on SNS sites like Facebook, twitter on customer behavior. Now in the technological edge social media is powerful tool and influencing the customer behavior and shaping the perception about product and services. For understanding the fact related hypothesis and practice, different International and national Literature review has been investigated and assessed.

The entire purpose of this research is to consider and analyze the effect of social media advertisement on SNS sites like Facebook, twitter on customer behavior. Now in the technological edge social media is powerful tool and influencing the customer behavior and shaping the perception about product and services. For understanding the fact related hypothesis and practice, different International and national Literature review has been investigated and assessed.

The challenges and opportunities of Social Media, has defined Social Media as a group of Internet-based applications that is built on ideological and technological foundations of Web 2.0 and that allow the creation and exchange of User Generated Content. The writer of the paper has explained that although Social Media is a related concept, with Web 2.0 and User Generated Content and has evolved from the same, however it differs from them on technological and ideological grounds. The various types of Social Media tools or applications like Collaborative projects, blogs, content communities, social networking sites, virtual game worlds and virtual social worlds are explained in detail. The author says that today everything is about social media and that if you do not participate in Face-book, YouTube, Twitter you are no more a part of cyberspace. Social media is a tool through which businesses can directly contact the end-consumers, within short span of time and with great efficiency and that too at low cost as compared to other traditional media. This paper recommends companies, for developing their own Social Media strategies in order to be a part of this new trend and gain more profits.

Afendi H. (2012) in Social Media : The new hybrid element of the promotion mix, argues that Social Media is a hybrid element of the promotion mix because in a traditional sense it enables companies to talk to their customers, while in a non-traditional sense it enables customers to talk directly to one another. The writers feel that Social Media being a hybrid element of the promotional mix, should be incorporated as an integral part of the company's Integrated Marketing Communication (IMC). When Procter and Gamble (P&G) or General Electric (GE) entered the arena of Social Media, they carefully framed their communications with the market place in order to consistently reflect their organizational values and they acknowledge the value of incorporating Social Media into their IMC strategies and promotional efforts. The second promotion related role of Social media is : customers can use Social Media to communicate with one another. The organization cannot control the content, timing, and frequency of the social media based conversations occurring between consumers. This stands in contrast to the traditional integrated marketing communications paradigm where organizations have a high degree of control over the customer's communication. The Social Media has profoundly affected all aspects of consumer behaviour, and has bestowed consumers with power they have not previously experienced.

Andreas, K. (2011) in the social media revolution, says that the impact of Social Media is being felt across the globe. Social Media has changed the manner in which the communication between the organizations and the customers were taking place; it has changed from talking through mass media to listening and conversing through social media. Since the consumer online is a commentator, reviewer and publisher, all the organizations have to stop talking and start listening to how they are perceived online. Listening is just the start, after listening, actively participating in the discussions with the consumers and engaging them is crucial. This engagement with the consumers online will be the key way for building long-term advocates of the brand, who not only purchase their products but also recommend them on and offline. The writer then opines that there is a huge opportunity for research, as the need for research outputs and knowledge will shape the consumer opinion. Research and research companies have a great scope for research through Social Media and the research companies that evolve with Social Media can increasingly prosper. Research Companies can evolve in various ways :Build community : Consumers want to share views and opinion and communities should grab this opportunity and tap in. This means providing constant surveys, message boards, listening permanently and not occasionally, and making the conversation two-way by sharing results back with them.

Bhatt, S. (2012) in her research paper writes about the emergence of Social Media, the whole communications landscape has transformed and the mass mobilizing power of Social Media is tremendous. People think that Social Media is a threat to traditional PR and mainstream media, however Social media complements traditional PR and traditional PR will exist as an important component of any successful business. The PR and advertising agencies are all undergoing a change and are trying to evolve their strategy, physical structure and business models to be in tune with social media. The PR audience interacts with the content differently and usually in a passive way, whereas the social media audience is more engaging and interactive. Author described the result that social media being more two-sided than PR which is often seen as one-sided. Content put out for PR simply goes out to the audience with little or no engagement.

Bartikowski, S. (2012) in their study millennial use of online social networking sites-a uses and gratifications perspective have made an attempt to find out the reason behind millennial use of social networking site with special reference to bebo. The results of the study indicate that the participants were using bebo for their personal motives and in order to maintain a certain persona and identity in social context. The impersonal nature of the Social media has led to facilitate the millennial where they can negotiate the practicalities and forge the identities and maintain relationships. The study details why and how product reviews from consumer opinion platforms affect individual users' brand buying behavior. Drawing on social theories, the authors predict that consumers' perceptions of other consumers' product reviews affect brand buying intentions through two intervening variables: product- and brand-related attitudes. Moreover, the authors investigate whether these relationships are contingent on user type. The empirical results support a multiple mediation framework in which product- and brand attitudes mediate the effects of consumer product reviews on individual brand buying intentions.

Botha, E.(2011) in their study on Media Richness in Online Consumer Interactions : An Exploratory Study of Consumer-Opinion Web Sites have exclusively discussed on Consumer Opinion websites which provide opportunities to people to share their opinions or views about a product or service, read others opinions and also interact with other consumers. The writers have identified three major challenges which the consumer opinion websites face and they are quality of contributions, motivating users to participate and . Earning reader's trust. The main objective of this article is to find out ways by which the quality of the contents of these websites is enhanced so that it becomes a useful source of information for the consumers as well as the companies. The conclusions drawn from the study shows that the consumer opinion websites are more influential and provide more valuable information when they separate the complex task of information search and dissemination from the simple task of social interaction, and support each task with appropriate levels of richness. The writers conclude that consumers should consider both positive and negative points about a product or service before stating their opinion.

Bhatt, A. (2012) in his paper on Blog Popularity and Activity on Social Media: An Exploratory Research has made an attempt to find out the impact of some social media website's popularity on ROI. Social media provides a global opportunity for brands to use them as an effective channel for marketing of products and services. However the effectiveness of any marketing channel is largely dependent on a very important entity the ROI. ROI is something that most marketers look at when one has to determine the effectiveness of any marketing channel. The study therefore examined ROI for weblogs and how their promotions through two highly popular social networking sites, namely Facebook and Twitter affects their popularity and in turn increases their revenue through advertisements. Page views is a direct measure of the traffic a particular blog has and therefore a correlation between page views and Facebook fans and twitter fans was established to understand the effect of promotion of brands through social media. The findings of the study revealed a positive correlation across all blog categories and hence it was concluded that a positive change in Facebook followers and Twitter followers increases the number of page views. It was also found that the page views increased with the increase in time due to an increase in fans or followers.

Bhatt A.(2013) in their research paper Factors influencing Online Shopping : An Empirical Study in Ahmadabad writes about the factors which influence the perceptions of consumers regarding online shopping. The study has revealed ease/attractiveness of website, service quality of websites and website security as the three important factors which have prominently emerged from the study. The paper has proved that that these factors are related to specific type of consumers classified as occasional, frequent and regular consumers. The study shows that the regular buyers are most influenced by the ease/attractiveness and service quality of website, whereas the occasional buyers value website security to a greater extent.

Chu,S. (2011) in their study on role of social networking sites in some key cases throws a light on the growing popularity of social networking sites. The study showed that people have got their own media to raise their voice and stand for their rights. Author thinks that Social Media possess the character of true democratization of information. Study concludes that the participatory nature of Social Networking Sites cuts through caste and class barriers.

Chung,J. (2013) in their study The Social Media and Entrepreneurship Growth focused on the effect of social media on the growth of SMEs in Nairobi. The study established that social media tools offer greater market accessibility and CRM which in turn have a significant impact on the growth of SMEs. This study recommends that the policy makers should come up with favorable internet surfing rates and e-business policies to encourage the technological adoption that would grow the SME industry.

Efthymious,C. (2009), examines the possibilities of different sections of society following different trends of communication. This study talks about the usage of product promotion on social media, by the multinational companies in India especially in the FMCG sector.

Erkon (2011) in the research paper "The Use of Social Networking Sites among Malaysian university students". The millennial most often use social media to interact and socialize with their peers. This study is conducted nationwide in Malaysia, where SNSs are popular and very commonly used for interaction by the millennial, however there is very limited data available on the patterns of its use for the wider segment of the target population. The results show that the SNS has not penetrated completely i.e. 100% in Malaysia as was assumed earlier. The study also shows that the respondents are found to spend more time on interacting and socializing through SNS than learning and they do not think that the use of SNS affects their academic performance. It has come out from the studies that the respondents are using SNS for the purpose of informal learning activities and nearly half i.e. 50.3% use it to get in touch with the lecturers for informal learning purpose.

Hawkins (2011) done an exploratory study of university brand visibility in social media. Brands are using Social Media to acquire new customers and to retain the existing ones. Brands need to acquire information about their visibility on these social networking sites, as compared to the visibility of their competitors. This is an exploratory study that has been conducted on the South African University brands. This study has identified, positioning of the brands over social media and the strategies followed by them to make themselves visible to the audience, as the tools for knowing the visibility of the brands. The findings of the study revealed that the South African University brands do not have a distinct position over social media, nor do they have effective strategies to engage their stakeholders. The writers concluded that the institutions should have a fair attitude towards Social media, since social media is currently governing the internet and the media. The people who are managing these brands can see this as an opportunity to make the brand presence prominent.

Jagongo (2013) in their paper "Effectiveness of Social Networking Sites (SNS)" have made an attempt to figure out the experiences of the internet users regarding social media and have also tried to find out the pattern of SNS usage of the consumers. The writers state that social media has become so much popular, that it has surpassed the popularity of email, to become number four after search, portals and PC software applications. The tremendous increase in the amount of time people are spending using these SNS have changed the way people spend their time online and this affects the way people behave, interact and share in their normal daily lives. This paper has tried to analyze the overall effectiveness of SNS.

Janukareg (2012) in their research study "Effective use of Social Websites towards business among academicians and students". The study lists the benefits of social websites for business: 1. To create brand awareness. 2. Utility of SNSs as an effective online reputation management tool. 3. For the purpose of recruiting. 4. To learn about new technologies and competitors. 5. As a lead generation tool to intercept potential prospects. The results of the study reveals that most of professionals and students are aware about business taking place through social networking sites, however most of them are not using it for the business purpose. Most of the respondents are using SNSs for socializing. Therefore the writers think that the social websites need to grab the professionals and students from rural areas to concentrate on business through Social websites.

Johnksion (2009) in their research study "Social Media: A New Frontier for Retailers" This study has proposed number new strategies for retailers implementing which will not only help the retailers to survive, but create a competitive advantage and flourish in the new environment.

Karve (2013) in their research work "The fairyland of Second Life: Virtual social worlds and how to use them". At the beginning this study the authors have discussed about the evolution of virtual social worlds and its history. Followed by how it fits in our time and lastly how they are different from other social media, such as content communities (e.g. YouTube), social networking sites and blogs (e.g. Facebook), collaborative projects (e.g. Wikipedia) and virtual game worlds. This study has thrown light on how businesses can make use of these virtual social worlds in the field of advertising and communication, virtual product sales (v-Commerce), human resource, marketing research and internal process management. Along with it this study has also discussed increasing linkages between the real and the virtual worlds, enforcement of law and order and transformation of virtual social business as business hubs or centers of the future.

Kevin (2014) in their research "Privacy as information access and illusory control : The case of the Facebook News feed privacy outcry". A survey was conducted on 172 current Facebook users in one of the large universities of US in order to determine the reasons and the extent to which the users were upset and to investigate the influence of the News feed privacy outcry on the user behaviour changes. The results showed that an easy access to information and an unreal loss of control which was alerted by the introduction of News feed features stimulates, privacy and security concerns among users.

Logon,J. (2013) in their research study "Exploring the impact of Culture in Social Media Sphere : A content analysis of non-profit organization's use of Facebook". A content analysis of 225 non-profit organization's Facebook profiles was carried out for the research purpose. Particularly the study has focused on the ways in which the organizations disclose information about themselves and about those who manage their Facebook presence, ways of promoting the organizational accomplishments and news, and engaging with the stakeholders in relation to their context, performance and collectivist/individualist natures, respectively. The findings of the study showed mixed support for the impact of traditional cultural expectations, thus suggesting that global connectivity of social media may be contributing to blurred cultural boundaries in favor of virtual culture that promoted the global community.

Buhalis, C. (2012) in their research study " Social Media as a destination marketing tool: its use by national tourism organizations". Social media are gaining more importance in the marketing strategies of DMOs as it helps in seeking greater value in the way marketing budgets are spent. Social media offers DMOs with global audience at limited costs. The writer has made an attempt to determine the impact and usage of social media marketing strategies and has developed a model of best practices for the national tourism organizations to learn from. The findings show that the social media usage among the top DMOs is still experimental and the strategies differs extensively.

Kevin,K. (2014) in their research work "Social media technology usage and customer relationship performance: A capabilities-based examination of social CRM". This paper has made an attempt to conceptualize and measure the capabilities of social CRM. The second important contribution of this paper is exploring how social CRM capabilities are influenced by customer centric management systems and social media technologies. The results suggests that social media technologies and customer centric management systems had a positive relation with the customer relationship performance.

Bhukya (2012) in the research paper "Presence of Indian Big IT Brands on Social Media : an Empirical Study". The data for this study has been collected from the respective brand's social media websites and analyzed on a 5 point scale. The research findings shows that HCL and Infosys have high scores of 3.75 points for their social media presence and have their brand accounts on 7 social network sites each. Next with score of 1.75 and presence on 7 SNS is Wipro followed by TCS with score of 1.25 and social media presence on 6 SNS. de Vries et.al. (2012) conducted a study on 355 brand posts from 11 international brands spread across six categories of products and the result shows that positioning the brand post on top of the brand fan page helps in increasing and enhancing the popularity of the brand post. The author opines that the SNS are free to join because if they are not free they will not expand and earn money from the brand or customer driven advertisements.

Social media has opened the doors of global markets and Infosys, Wipro, HCL and TCS are now preparing to compete with the global biggies. Already Indian companies have labor availability at comparatively much lower costs as compared to the global companies which is one advantage that the Indian companies have in their favor. However value created in the fields of brand, intellectual property will take these Indian companies to new heights. Accordingly these tech companies are working aggressively over budgets for marketing globally, enhancing global positioning and brand valuations.

Schultz (2009) in their research work "IMC: New horizon/false dawn for a marketplace in turmoil". The writers argue for a totally new opinion for IMC going forward to match the economic realities faced by the organizations. IMC will be driven by marketplace, customer, technological changes enhanced by globalization and a shift of marketplace power to consumers, all heavily influenced by the current economic conditions.

Nile (2010) in "The lasting effects of Social Media Trends on Advertising" has explored that there is no use investing millions in traditional methods of advertising because people find new ways to block or get away from these advertisements. The key is to target the right people with the right messages. In order to do this, the marketers should focus on Connectors(are the ones that move and steer people into directions and avenues of interest to them) , Mavens(are the ones who want to know the best deals and tell everyone about it) and salespeople(who have the ability to convince and sell new ideas). The connectors, mavens and salespeople have the ability to give a high return on investment, since by targeting them the organization can acquire high sales just by targeting a small group of people. Thus targeting the right people not only brings down the organization's advertising expenses but also drastically improves their marketing productivity. Social Media makes it very easy for any organization to connect with these connectors, mavens and salespeople. It is very important to use holistic, comprehensive relationship marketing strategy to target these people, since they are key drivers in influencing the consumers buying decision. To build and sustain such a relationship, marketers must understand and respond to customer needs and goals. Marketers are using tailored social networking forums to reach the consumers in a more personalized way. Marketers are finding that interactive and targeted marketing are the key to success and are far more beneficial than the traditional advertising.

Lynne (2011) in their research work "Evidence of IMC in social marketing". This research study has given evidence of IMC being successfully incorporated in the communication of school-based health promotion activities within schools that promotes health. The findings of the research reveals that IMC principles are successfully communicated and forms part of the HPS(health promoting school) policy of promoting health. This research throws light on how IMC can and should be used in social marketing. This research has provided insights for social marketing practitioners to improvise on the communication efforts.

Tan (2013) in paper "The Antecedents of Effectiveness Interactive Advertising in the Social Media" have tried to find out consumer's attitude towards interactive advertising and its impact on purchase intention. Through their study the writers have made an attempt to share some understandings and opinions with advertisers and companies on the measurement of effectiveness, which they can consider when placing an interactive advertising. In the literature review the writers states the following factors as the determinants of the effectiveness of interactive advertising: Attitude towards Advertising, Attitude towards Advertised Brand, Purchase Intention, Time of exposure to advertisement. The results of the study reveal that, there is a positive relation between attitude towards advertisement and purchase intention to effectiveness of interactive advertising. Thus the writers concluded saying traditional advertising could be used, but interactive advertising measures should be an add on.

Guang (2012) in his research paper "The effectiveness of advertising through the social media in Gauteng" has made an attempt to investigate the effectiveness of advertising through the medium of social media and has focused mainly on Facebook. The author states that social media marketing explores and utilizes the social aspect of the web and is therefore able to connect and interact on a much more personalized manner than the traditional marketing.

The study reveals brand engagement, brand attitude, brand image and consumer engagement as the factors contributing to the effectiveness of advertising. The paper also talks about brands having strong market presence automatically getting more attention from consumers on Social media. The author concludes that in order to be effective, a brand needs to be established and must have strong brand reputation. The advertisements on Facebook serve to supplement the brand and does not put the brand up the rank in terms of its reputation.

Erkon (2011) in their research paper "Analysis of social networking strategy in developing brand communication", with the primary objective of determining the effectiveness of brand communication strategy in advertising products and promoting brands on social networking sites. The various reasons for social media being a widely used platform, for advertising compared to the other traditional advertising mediums have been discussed. The various ways that are being provided by social media platform for its users to communicate with each other and interact with the brand are discussed like chat, messaging, video, email, voice chat, file-sharing, blogging and discussion groups. According to the writers views, the marketing communications are becoming personal, interesting, interactive and social. Findings of the study suggest that social media advertising has its impact on 70% of the users and half of them access these ads i.e. games, quiz, events etc. It was found that the interaction is more in the display banner advertisements in Face book and Orkut. Every Social networking site has a unique communication strategy and user interaction. Face book promote and allows user interactions, Twitter feeds posts relating the brand and Orkut promote through click ads and promotional brand pages. Face shows accessibility because of its huge popularity and Twitter gives more importance to the text. The writers concluded by stating that Social networking sites have the scope to grow big for highly targeted marketing and advertising. Social networking sites present enormous opportunities to build the brands and have become a branding hub.

Jothi (2012) in the research study " A study on online marketing strategies used by E-Entrepreneurs in India". The study has analyzed

E-Entrepreneurs like Amazon, Flip kart, Naaptol etc. for the purpose of studying the nature and extent of marketing strategies used by successful online Entrepreneurs. SNSs apart from being a fantastic medium of communication and interaction, keeps the customers informed of the consumer market as well. Through this paper the writers have voiced their view that there is a need to analyze and research the needs of the customers who come online to fulfill their requirements. Internet has given an opportunity to entrepreneurs to market their products and services across the globe and has opened the doors of such a gigantic market, that their sales force cannot even think of identifying. The online companies can engage in online promotional activities through effective online marketing strategies to enhance their offerings in the online markets. Advertising on the internet not only provides the information about the offerings but it also encourages innovation. The study concluded by revealing the results which stated that Social media marketing is one of the best online marketing strategies that has been used by the E-Entrepreneurs. The results also revealed that the International players like e.Bay.com, Amazon.com are well ahead in customer relationship building and management and in the online marketing strategies. Indian brands are identifying the strategies which the international websites use to improve the website and are trying to build their brand identity.

Ronald (2013) in their research the authors have expressed their opinion about the traditional advertising business being directly hit by direct marketing. The reasons for the diminishing business of traditional advertising have been attributed to the arrival of new technologies that have empowered the consumers. A new market has evolved which is more in capacity, interactive and multimedia in place of the traditional mass media. This new media advertising results in more producer-consumer interactions.

Kolari (2008) in their study discussed about the information ecology of social media and online communities. Social media systems such as photo- and link-sharing sites like YouTube etc., weblogs, online forums are estimated to generate one third of the new web contents. One prominent feature that distinguishes the "web 2.0" sites from the other web pages is that they are interlinked with other forms of network data. Their standard hyperlinks are enriched by social networks, comments, trackbacks, advertisement, tags, resource description framework (RDF) data and metadata. The writers conclude by stating that as the internet evolves, it changes the way in which the people interact with it as content providers or content consumers and the results will be more interesting mixture of underlying networks - network of individuals, groups, opinions, beliefs, documents, advertisements and scams. These interwoven networks will pose new opportunities and challenges for extracting information and knowledge from them.

Florian (2011) in his research work "Predicting User's future level of communication activity in online social networks: A first step towards more advertising effectiveness". To enable effectiveness of advertising strategies, identifying a user who can influence a large number of friends or acquaintances is essential. In this regards, the user's future level of online communication activity in online social network plays an important role. High online activity in the past does not guarantee high level of the future online activity. The means of predicting user's future level of communication activity are required. Therefore the writers have proposed a probability based model that has been developed to primarily forecast the purchasing behaviour of the consumers resulting from the user's communication activity on online social networks.

Bartikowski (2010) in their research paper Attitude contagion in consumer opinion platforms: posters and lurkers have tried to explain how consumer's perception about product reviews affect the product and brand attitudes and in turn affect the consumer's buying decision. This study also reveals how the consumer product reviews affect the brand-related attitudes of posters than lurkers.

Borges (2012) in their study "The effectiveness of social marketing mix strategy : Towards an Anthropological Approach". The author has described social marketing as a new science that seeks to improve the overall life quality of human beings by adopting marketing strategies and skills without aiming for making profits. Although the basic concepts of social marketing and commercial marketing are similar, however their principles differ in various fields. The author feels that the social marketers should become aware of the anthropological aspect of social marketing and about the differences between the social and commercial marketing theories. Social marketers should be able to apply anthropological theories and methods into social marketing practice.

Kashia (2012). Different media of marketing before social media revolution have been discussed, followed by the evolution of Social media. The impact of social media on marketing is discussed in detail with the help of standard metrics like online advertising, public relations and search engine optimization. The paper has also discussed the concerns and criticism of social media. Some of the important concerns were if the customers post comments or tweets in haste it can cause severe damage to the brand image. If the consumers find the brand's social networking activity intrusive then there is a high risk of losing the consumer. Since marketers are directly dealing with the public, they cannot lurk behind the scene, but have to become more accountable for the brand. The growing popularity of social media can lead to social media overtaking to other functional areas of marketing. Social media is building a bridge between the marketers and the consumers through continuous engagement, building trust and targeting the right audience at the right time and in real-time.

Jothi (2011) in their exploratory research work have tried to determine the students pattern of using social media and social networking sites in relation to their reactions to the advertisements on social media, where they have the freedom to choose the information they engage with. The aim of this research paper is to empirically investigate what type of social media users, have a positive outlook regarding advertising on social networking sites. This study has contributed to the existing knowledge, of consumer behaviour in an online environment and on developing positive reactions to online advertisements and have also presented new ways to classify the online consumers, which served as a basis for psychographic segmentation, based on respondents online activities. The authors concluded stating that in order to be successful in the social media environment, companies must undergo continuous online marketing research and should be sensitive to the changes in consumer behaviour patterns and should be able to identify new areas of customer interest.

Hays (2012) in paper Facebook versus television: advertising value perceptions among females the writers compared the perceptions of female students regarding value of advertising on social network sites and value of advertising on television. Advertising trustworthiness-The study shows that consumers have become more concerned about the factualness or trustworthiness of advertising content. It was found out that consumer-generated product recommendations are more recommended than marketer- generated product recommendations. Involvement-SNSs provide an involving environment for advertisers. The users of Social networking sites involve in brand related activities and are therefore more engaged than consumers who simply read, listen or watch advertisements about a brand. Advertising effectiveness measures-It was found out that the advertisements having an element of entertainment and information in them are more accepted advertisements on SNSs. The results indicated that the millennial crowd (19-24) is more inclined towards in formativeness than entertainment and millennial participants are more engaged by entertaining advertisements on SNSs. Therefore it was concluded that informativeness and entertainment play a significant role in assessing advertising value whereas irritation did not play a significant role in assessing the advertising value.

Gupta (2013) in the research paper assessing the Influence of Social Media on Consumer's Purchase Intentions has made an attempt to determine the impact of social media on product evaluation and the resulting decision-making process of Indian consumers. The results are supportive of the fact that social media does affect purchase intentions. More Specifically, there is a positive and strong impact of three factors namely peer communication, perceived product informativeness and the level of product involvement on consumers purchase intentions in the context of social media. The author concludes that as the products offered online cannot be examined, perceived information on social media and its spread through communication among peer groups facilitates consumer's evaluation and purchase related decision.

Karve (2013) in their research paper "The emergence of the social media empowered consumer" has thrown a light upon the various platforms that has an impact on traditional relationship marketing concepts and how this has resulted in raising consumer expectations of the conventional business. This study also talks about areas like word of mouth and consumer empowerment and emphasizes the areas of potential development in theory and practice as a result of social media empowerment. The author in this study has expressed his views about social media and CRM. He says that Social media has completely changed the manner in which communication takes place thereby giving a new dynamics to the human relationships. The organizations which are accepting social media must also accept that they are losing the element of control to the consumers. For most of the businesses social media has gained a lot of importance in establishing their web presence overtaking the company website and email communication programme. This has completely changed the manner in which the organizations are interacting with their consumers and how they are implementing the customer relationship management strategies. The main difference between the traditional CRM and social CRM is that the social CRM is more customer oriented and it involves customers proactively. The author also talks about word of mouth marketing that empowers the organization and not the consumer.

Methew (2009) in their research paper Consumer Behaviour in Social Networking Sites: Implications for Marketers have made an attempt to investigate whether social networking sites (SNSs) can be used as an effective tool of marketing and whether it can engage the consumers to participate in marketing on SNSs. The authors write that companies need to undertake a different approach that will attract consumers rather than pushing marketing messages on them. If marketing messages are pushed onto the consumers it will result in adverse reaction and the consumers will express their dissatisfaction when they are communicating over SNS. This will have a negative effect on the company and put an end to the potential of SNS to be used as a marketing tool. This paper talks about developing the correct approach in using SNSs as a marketing tool. In this paper the authors have drawn a conclusion that companies need to work towards having a 'friendship' based approach with the consumers and need to build relationships with them in order to have the SNSs act as a Marketing tool for the companies.

Philip (2009) in their study "An empirical study on shopping tendency through social networking sites (SNSs)". Different methods of payment used for shopping through SNSs are focused in this study. This research study has revealed that social networking sites have different target consumers and factors; and have correlated these factors. The nature of the study is exploratory since it focuses on new idea of virtual shopping through SNSs. The writers opine that patrons who vary in age all through the 30s are captivating the targets for sellers of goods and accommodations. The writer further states that due to the unique characteristics of gregarious networks the items that are sold on the gregarious networking sites can vary from the items that are being sold on other virtual sites. The internet sites largely sell authentic items i.e. the items (goods or accommodation) that can be used offline, irrespective of whether they are bought online or offline, such as books, flight tickets, furniture, apparel etc. The gregarious networks not only sell authentic items but they additionally sell virtual items i.e. the items (good or accommodations) whose use and purchase are constrained by exacting web space, such as homepage outline, avatars, implicit gifts, music that can be utilized only on concrete websites etc. The findings of the study shows that time spent on social destinations is a differentiating element that influence the disposition to looking for things on a long range interpersonal communication. The apparent fit is the strongest factor that influence the shopping intensions on social destinations. The study found out that the individuals who regularly use long range informal communication locales usually accept more extra offers. Therefore the informal community clients hesitate to shop on interpersonal communication locales. It has been discovered through this study that different age groups have association with the SNS shopping variable. From the managerial viewpoint the study reveals that the target consumers and the features of SNSs should differ according to the product type if SNSs look forward to expand their businesses to include the shopping services. That is millennial with positive perceptions of usefulness, ease of use and security of shopping services on SNSs.

Smith (2010) in their study "Determinants of consumer engagement in electronic word-of-mouth (eWOM) in social networking sites". As more and more marketers incorporate social media in their promotional activities, there is a need to investigate the determinants that impact the consumers engagement in eWOM via social networks. eWOM is based on three aspects : opinion seeking behaviour, opinion giving behaviour and opinion passing behaviour. Opinion seekers depend on others advice to make purchase decision. Opinion givers exert a great influence on others opinions. Opinion passers help in the flow of information. Literature review has revealed four social relationship variables - tie strength, homophile, trust and interpersonal influence. Interpersonal influence is further divided into normative influence and informational influence. The results indicate that tie strength, trust, normative and informational influence had a positive relationship with all types of eWOM behaviors. However homophile had a negative relationship with the eWOM behaviour.

Richard (2012) in their research work about shopping on social networking websites and attitudes toward real versus virtual items. The study is based on two types of products which are present on social networking sites: Real products and Virtual products. The study reveals that usefulness, age, ease of use, security and fit play a significant role in determining the attitude for shopping real products. On the other hand gender, social networking site experience, ease of use and fit influence the attitudes for shopping virtual products.

Sarah (2011) in their study "An examination of the factors influencing consumer's attitudes towards social media marketing". Consumer communities on social media are new marketplaces for marketers. The goal of this research is to identify the factors that affect the consumer's attitude towards marketing on a social media platform.

Tom (2013) in their research work "To be or not to be in social media : How brand loyalty is affected by social media?". The study has aimed to show how brand communities based on social media influence the elements of customer centric model (i.e. the relationships between focal customer and brand, product, company and other customers) and brand loyalty. An empirical study was conducted on 441 respondents through survey method. The results of the study revealed that brand communities present on social media have a positive effect on customer-product, customer-brand, customer- Company and customer-other customer relationships, these in turn have positive effect on brand trust and trust has positive effect on brand loyalty. The study found that brand trust plays an intermediary role in converting the effects of relationships in brand community to brand loyalty.

Vinerean (2013) in their research work "Understanding consumer's responses toward social media advertising and purchase intention towards luxury products. The popularity of Social media as an advertising platform is increasing with the users interacting with each other and with the brand. In the same time period the online luxury market experienced enormous growth due to rising number of users in the age group of 18-35 and belonging to affluent background. This research focused on determining millennial social media user's belief, attitudes and behavioral response towards social media advertising. Brand consciousness and awareness was found to have its effect on user's attitudes towards social media advertising, which eventually affects their behavioral response towards social media advertising and ultimately affects purchase intention of luxury products.

Veran (2016) in their research paper "Consumer electronics vertical Focus : The heights of invention" has stated that consumer electronics sector has been the first sector in experimenting and trying out the different techniques of digital marketing. The various product promotional campaigns taken up on the Social Media by the digital pioneers like Sony, Toshiba, Samsung, Panasonic and the overwhelming responses they received online form a part of this paper. It has been put forth by the writers that the key challenge faced by the consumer electronics brands has been to effectively communicate the complexity of their products to a wide audience and through digital marketing they have overcome this challenge and therefore they are turning to digital marketing. Online video and Social Media (Social media includes Consumer reviews, online communities and forums) have been cited as the greatest opportunities by the consumer electronics brands. The brands can directly open a dialogue with the consumer, understand the consumer's needs, answer their questions, get feedback and have a friendly engagement with the consumer; all because of Social Media.

Veankteshwaran (2012) in their research work has been defined as the electronic word of mouth in which some marketing messages relating to the product, or brand is transmitted in an exponentially growing way through social media applications. This study has considered three conditions which need to be fulfilled to create an epidemic of viral marketing. These three conditions are giving the right message to the right messengers in the right environment. For any business there are two main reasons of using the social media platform .

Wright (2010) in their research work "Television meets Facebook: Social Networks through Consumer Electronics". The project consists of an IP enabled digital video recorder in the form of advance cable television set-top box connected to Facebook social network. The objective of this project are : a. How can the omnipresent consumer electronics work together in a simple way, b. How can the data available on social networking application diffuse in useful ways into the participant's real lives and c. How can these systems accomplish these tasks seamlessly without adding time or complexity to the user's experience? The results of this project are the user can now watch on his TV, the media that his friends enjoy, as well as his own explicitly requested recordings, through the system of ratings the user can use her DVR's enhanced interface to post back on social network what shows have been liked by them. The user's profile box in Facebook is going to be the main tool for sharing the user's upcoming viewing schedule. The information on their profile affects their viewing habits; therefore users will be more conscious with whom they add in their friend network and what information they provide through their profiles. The integration of consumer electronics and social networking is expected to benefit the content producers and distributors through the automation of word-of-mouth (WOM) recommendation. This project is also expected to help the users in finding the appealing new content faster than they would otherwise, help users in sharing contents and experiences more easily and will help the content distributors track content distribution in a social network directly into consumer electronics.

Chapter 3

Research Methodology

GLIMPSE OF RESEARCH

Title	IMPACT OF SOCIAL MEDIA ADVERTISEMENTS ON BUYING BEHAVIOUR OF MILLANNIAL IT PROFESSIONALS FOR ELECTRONIC GADGETS
Research Design	Descriptive
Population	Our target population is millennial Information Technology Professionals working in the IT companies in Indore in the age group of 18-35(millennial).
Sample Size	514
Data Collection	Structured Questionnaires
Research Tools	SPSS VERSION17 RESEARCH TOOLS Frequency Table With percentages Analysis of Variance (ANOVA) Chi-Square Test Regression Rank Order

3.1   The Study

The study has been conducted in two phases. Initially in Phase-I, Exploratory research has been conducted. For the same purpose formal interactions were conducted with those millennial working IT professional, who use online sites for buying consumer electronics products. After the interactions, the variables of the study had been identified and accordingly the questionnaire was prepared. In Phase-II, a Descriptive study had been conducted. The secondary data had been collected from various available resources. Review of Literature from various published reports, research journals, reference books and online databases.

3.2   The Design

The study was conducted in Indore. The sample unit is IT professional in the age group of 18-35 .Random sampling technique has been used for this study. In a Random sample from infinite population selection of each item is controlled by the same probabilities and the successive selections are independent of one another.

3.3   The Sample design

3.3.1. Reliability
The value of chronbah's Alpha found around 0.786 and the reliability limit is 0.6, so Questionnaire is reliable.
3.3.2   Size and Design of Sample
The research conducted in Indore (Madhya Pradesh). The sample group is millennial in the age accumulation of 18-35 and in information technology profession.
3.3.3. Sampling Technique:
Random Sampling method used in this research. In this sampling method infinite population selection is controlled by same probability and the selection are independent to one another.

Formula used for calculating the sample size.

$$n = \left[\frac{z_{\alpha/2}\sigma}{E} \right]^2$$

n = Sample size , σ = Standard Deviation, E = Margin of Estimated Error

$z_{\alpha/2}$ = is the critical value and the critical

value is $z_{\alpha/2}$ = 1.96.

The margin of error for this equation $E = 1$ and the used standard deviation $\sigma = 18.19$.

Using the formula for sample size, n:514 respondents is required for sample size

Table 3.1: Sample Size

Place	Respondents
Indore	514
TOTAL	514

3.4   Tools for Data Collection

The data collected from questionnaire were scored and tabulated into a master data sheet. The data was analyzed with the help of statistical package SPSS 17. The mean scores arrived are put to various statistical analysis using various statistical tools in order to test the research hypothesis. The statistical tools applied included Chi-Square test, Regression, Anova, Rank Order Co-efficient etc.

The Data Analysis has been divided into:

Descriptive Analysis - The descriptive analysis has been written in the Annexure and can be referred to in the Annexure.

Inferential Analysis - Exclusive analysis has been done for the purpose of the research and the essence of the analysis has been presented in this chapter.

Analysis of Data :

The data was analyzed in SPSS version 17 using different statistical tools viz:

- ➢ Frequency Table With percentages
- ➢ Analysis of Variance (ANOVA)
- ➢ Chi-Square Test
- ➢ Regression
- ➢ Rank Order

The raw data has been collected from primary source i.e. with the help of questionnaire which consists of the question at two different levels of measurements i.e. nominal and interval scale.

To draw the logical inferences from the data descriptive and inferential statistics techniques had been used. The type of statistical techniques i.e. Bivariate analysis and Multivariate analysis has been used based upon the level of measurements of the questions pertaining to those variables. The Multivariate procedures dealing with the analysis of variance were used to test and to draw the inference whether the samples have been drawn from more than two populations having the same mean; it helped the researcher to understand the perception of the responses for all the factors in more than two groups. Then in bi- variety analysis, Chi square test has been used to find the association between the two qualitative variables. Frequency table with percentages has been used to identify the demographics and buying behaviour perception of millennial. Regression analysis has been used to determine the nature of relationship (functional relationship) between the variables of the study for forecasting or prediction. Rank Order has been used to determine which Social networking tool from Facebook, Twitter and LinkedIn is the most effective social networking tool. Rank Order correlation coefficient measures the strength of association between two ranked variables.

3.5   Statement of the Problem:

Social Media advertisement is the new area for marketing and brand promotion policy. Strategy and they can select the advertising media according to the effectiveness.

Now the information technology professionals especially millennial change the environment of online working. Therefore all the companies try to increase the presence on the social media platform by social media advertisement or user account in different social networking websites like Facebook, twitter, LinkedIn.

This is the main reason for expansion of different social networking sites and now most of the customer is online user, so companies also increasing the presence on social platform.

The main reason of selection of this topic is basically a personal interest in social networking sites and fast expansion and also desire to find out the relation between social media advertisement and buying behavior of millennial in the area of consumer electronics.

A literature review also revealed that there is not much work on impact of social media advertisement on millennial in consumer electronics segment.

The impacts of the social media advertisements on Buying Behaviour of Millennial with special Reference to Information Technology Professional for Electronic Gadgets are the main objective of the study.

3.6   Objectives:

After the literature review, gap identified about impacts of the social media advertisements on buying behavior of millennial and according to this objective of the study was framed.

The main objective of research work is broken down into the following measurable objectives:

- To study various determinants influence the buying behavior of Millennial on social media advertising.
- To analyzed drivers, motives, reasons and factors affecting the buying behaviors of Millennial.
- To study theme and appeal which influence the buying behavior of Millennial
- To study cultural and geographical forces on Social media advertisement.
- To study the impact of social media advertisement on perception of Millennial while they purchase electronic gadgets.

3.7   Hypothesis:

From the Objectives of the study the following Hypothesis were formed: H_01: There is no specific reason of consumer's social media usage.

Hypothesis:

H01. There is no significant impact of social media advertisement on buying behavior of millennial.

H11. There is significant impact of social media advertisement on buying behavior of millennial.

H02   There is no significant impact of age on buying behavior of millennial.

H12   There is no significant impact of age on buying behavior of millennial.

H03   There is no significant impact of income on buying behavior of millennial.

H13   There is significant impact of income on buying behavior of millennial

H04   There is no significant impact of gender on buying behavior of millennial.

H14   There is significant impact of gender on buying behavior of millennial.

H05   There is no significant impact of education on buying behavior of millennial.

H15   There is significant impact of education on buying behavior of millennial.

H06   There is no significant impact of cultural and geographical forces on buying behavior of millennial.

H16   There is significant impact of cultural and geographical forces on buying behavior of millennial.

3.8   Methodology

In the analysis and finding of this proposed research these stages covered in the research methodology. Questionnaire, sample selection data collection, processing of collected data and assuredly analysis of the data. Qualitative analysis approaches used for the research finding analysis.

3.9   Study Limitation:

The study was conducted for impacts of the social media advertisements on buying behaviour of Millennial with special Reference to Information Technology Professional for Electronic Gadgets in Indore city for the millennial with special reference of information technology professional. So this study may not be acceptable everywhere because of social, economic and cultural differences.

Chapter 4

Social Networking Sites

4.1   Social Media Sites

Online Review is a tool of Social Media for empowerment of the customer and it has the high potential to increase the sales of a product or a brand and negative review can ruin the brand. Online review is basically any good or bad view fabricated by any customer or above barter about a product or company, which is available on the internet for other customer.

 Consumers generally give the very importance to the online review and customer feedback available on the online sites. At the time of purchasing the online review and rating of product is major factor for taking decisions. Yet online review can create problems for company also because company cannot control the public opinion and it can be damage the brand reputation. So properly management of online reviews and feedback is important task for the marketing managers.

Social media management (SMM) is the new field of management, which associate with the success and growth of the social media and for the present era, this is very important from marketing point of view.

In any industry now the online communication with the customer can be easily manage with the application of social media management and as well as the marketing activity at the smaller level also can be managed very efficiently.

SMM also help to manage and reorganize the views and comments of the company on the different online mediums like face book, twitter, different customers review websites and ultimately it provide the reflection of company policy and products update in the virtual world of social network.

SMM is an important tool for understanding and collecting the product review and can improve the product quality by proper feedback to the production and other departments. By proper management of social media, company can increase the presence in the different websites, blogs, and company websites and can attract at the mass level to the online user and whenever the online user will see the product then only customer can think about purchasing of the product.

4.1.1. Facebook

Facebook is the very popular and authentic social networking website, which invented by Mark Zuckerberg and his team members Eduardo Severing, Dustin Muscovite, and Chris Hughes in February 2004 by the starting name of Facemash.

Basically Facemash was software written by mark, in which any person who enter in the website and can compare the two photographs with comment of hot or not. So this was the starting of the Facebook website, after that mark registered the Facebook and firstly it was restricted to Harvard students but after that other universities and colleges also added in the Facebook. In 2005 the Facebook domain is registered and the Facebook is opened for all.

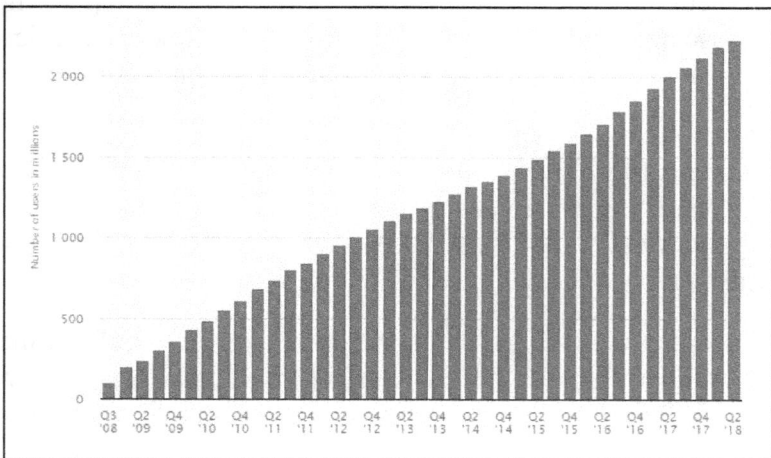

Figure 4.1: Numbers of user on Facebook

In terms of Facebook, if any user online within 30 days then it considered as active user of Facebook. Figure 4.1 shows the growth of Facebook from 2008 to 2018, in between this time the growth of Facebook was ultimate and gradually the Facebook enters in whole world except some restricted countries like china, North Korea.

As in the 2018, Facebook had around 2.23 billion active user and this user is the basis of the online social marketing platform because Facebook is the leader in social networking sites and this is the strength of online social networking media by which this online user can be convert into the customer of any product.

Facebook introduced paid advertisement services to the manufacturer and on the basis of customer choice and segmentation, Facebook also provide the personalized advertisement according to the interest and requirement of the customer. The online data is the source of analysis the customer behavior pattern.

Advantages of Facebook:

Facebook is free

From starting, Facebook providing free joining service to the customer and that is very important point for increasing the user on the Facebook. In other websites they provide some premium services but in Facebook all the content and all the services free to the customer. For manufacture and company Facebook provide paid service by company can provide online advertisements to the customer.

Facebook helps in Networking

Now Facebook is the medium of social networking, by the Facebook user can be connect with the old friends, school friends, relatives, colleagues based on the feature on groups. In Facebook by forming the groups user can interact with the same liking or same objective people for the different purpose. By the sharing of videos and photos user cant interact and share the memoires with each other.

Facebook facilitates Business

In 2018 more than 2.23 billion user active on the Facebook with different communities and different age groups. In the terms of marketing all the Facebook user are the customer of different products and Facebook provides the business opportunity to the advertiser by the selecting target group and future customer, personalized advertisement is possible on the Facebook. Now Facebook is more trustworthy website and customer believes on the advertisement and offer provides by the Facebook

Facebook video chat

Facebook also providing the video chat service by the two or more user can video chat without any physical boundaries and no cost associated with this service,. This service is very popular now days in between the youngsters. This service providing by the Facebook for the user and more than one user also can go for group video calling also, this feature is very unique and useful for the business purpose also.

Facebook as image and video hosting site

Facebook user can create the photo, video upload on their user account and can share with the friends and relatives; this data is secured by the privacy policy of Facebook. This feature provides unique status to the Facebook and basis for more users.

Facebook security

Facebook provide all safety features to the user so they can secure their account with privacy policy of the Facebook. Facebook continuously review the Facebook security concern and accordingly work. For user safety Facebook provide double authentication for login and alert on mail, in case of unauthorized use of unknown place.

Free Gaming and app store on Facebook

Now a day's Facebook gaming is very popular between the user, in Facebook games are Facebook user are interconnected and they can send the request to one another and can participate in the games.

Facebook games are related with the virtual life and very popular on the gaming platform on social networking sites.

Facebook for news

Now Facebook providing online newsfeed to the customer according to the requirement and interest of the customer Facebook collaborate different organizations for providing news across world.

Disadvantages of Facebook:
Like other things, in Facebook also have some disadvantages
Fake profiles and ids
Fake profile means person hiding the original identification and connecting with other user with fake name. This type of fake id normally using for fraud and other criminal purpose. Facebook is working on that part and trying to remove fake id on the basis of artificial intelligence.
Addicting nature of Facebook

Facebook is very organized website and user can busy on chat, video or any other function for the hours. So in the nature Facebook is very addictive and sometimes user at the office time also uses Facebook. This addictive nature of Facebook creating problems in human life.

Privacy issues

Sometime new user don't know the security features of Facebook and id can be hacked by other person and can be use , user identity for different purpose. So without all security concern using of the Facebook is quite difficult.

4.1.2. Twitter:

Origin of Twitter

Twitter is SMS based very innovative innovation of this century. Initially Twitter was invented on SMS mobile based platform but after some time converted into web based platform by Jack Dorsey in 2006 with the help of Noah Glass, Biz Rock and Evan Williams.

Advantages of Twitter

- Twitter provides free service to the companies for business through the tweets. Companies can identify the targeted customer and can send the message by twitter.
- Twitter also provide the facility for finding the customer through analysis of tweets and also the companies can find out the policy of competitor through the tweets.
- Twitter can be acclimated by businesses to accept the strategies of the competitors by afterward their tweets.
- Twitter allow every individual user to connect the group of user and by this can find out the customers on twitter
- It helps to companies to find out the customer as well as continues relationship with customer by twitters and also by quick response of twits companies can find out the customer feedback of customer and can act accordingly.

Disadvantages of Twitter

- In the twitter many fake id are available, so sometime it is difficult to finding the right person and chances of fraud is also there.
- It is very easy to involved twitter in communication with large group of peoples and relations but for use of twitter as business tool the goal should be clear

4.1.3. LinkedIn

LinkedIn is very useful and oldest website on the social networking platform, it is older than Facebook, YouTube and twitter. LinkedIn basically launched for professional network development by Reid Hoffman on 5 May 2003.

Benefits LinkedIn Brings for Business

LinkedIn very useful for business owner, HR professional, professionals, business development office and sales persons for professional network and expansion of the business.

Find Business Partners, Users and Service Providers

In the LinkedIn by the simple search user can be connect to specialist, professionals related to your requirement. In the recruitment also by the simple search suitable candidate can search by the website. It is also useful to find your business partner relates to your business and you can post any advertisement related to business.

Information Sharing

LinkedIn is also a problem solving tool. In forum if user will post any question or quires related to requirement then by expert user and other group of people give answer on the forum so anybody can get right advice from the LinkedIn without any cost. It is the best tool of LinkedIn for information and knowledge sharing.

A Blog Promotional Tool

Users of LinkedIn are able to create profile and sharing experience with other as well as LinkedIn promotes the blogs for sharing the experience and knowledge.

LinkedIn Recommendations

Recommendation is another very important tool of LinkedIn, by this any user can connect with business or representative. In recommendation user can ask any information related with product to company and can enquire about the partnership into the business and in LinkedIn or outside of the website company can contact to the concern person. This is very useful feature of LinkedIn for connect the existing customer as well as in searching of new customer.

LinkedIn for SEO

LinkedIn profiles getting high page ranking on the goggle and other search engine websites so if any customer or person searches about the individual or about company then the it will influence the people. Now LinkedIn also gives the sharing of Facebook and twitter content on LinkedIn as well as LinkedIn profile also searchable to all search engines and social networking websites so it is helpful for user and spreading the business on LinkedIn.

Starting groups:

This facility provided by the LinkedIn to create the group of related activity or customer of particular business. By this facility any user can send link of group to the website and website link also can share with LinkedIn profiles. This is also the problem solving and sharing the information about products and update news of product.

Advertisement:

LinkedIn provides the facility LinkedIn Ads, on which any user or business can give advertisements of the company and LinkedIn charge, will be on the basis of per click by another user. Now LinkedIn have more than 150million user and this is very large group of user and customer, so advertisements in LinkedIn very effective and useful.

4.1.4. YouTube

You tube is now the most accepted and famous websites for sharing the video and in 2018 largest content of video in YouTube website on different topics and different subjects. Previously no one single website was available where all video can watch and share so YouTube was invented by Chad Hurley for this purpose and now the YouTube working on different objectives and providing comfortable and ease to use facility to the customer.

The first video was flashed in YouTube was "Me at the zoo". In October 2006, Google acquired the YouTube and now YouTube working in 65 countries with more than 100 different languages.

Now you tube working on business and advertisement areas. On very popular and other video before starting or in between the advertiser can play ad according to the requirement and in YouTube one more facility is that after some time that is depend on the customer that they want to see advertisement or not otherwise they can skip the advertisement. Now on the YouTube companies can upload the product and company information and other user can access the information.

Now largest user visiting on the YouTube, which is approximately more than one billion and 6 billion hours users watching the video and 200 hours videos uploading every minutes on YouTube.

4.1.5 Really Simple Syndication (RSS)

RSS is basically short form of Really Simple Syndication. This is the simple way to update information regarding websites to the user. It is basically a computer program by which RSS update to user about any new updating in desired website because for every person that is not possible to go and check the latest updates on the website. So this work is very useful, in the case of watching the updates of websites.

4.1.6 Slide Share

Slide share is basically a collection of different presentation by uploading of the different user of the sites and by sharing everyone can see the presentations. It is the largest website for uploading, downloading and sharing of presentation of different subjects. It supports all the format like .pdf, .doc,.ppt and available on the websites, this presentation can be share on the LinkedIn and on the YouTube also.

Slide share have millions user and slide share provides the advertisement facility to the companies for interact with user.

Chapter 5

Data Analysis

5.1   Analysis of Data

The collected survey data were calculated and converted into excel sheet for further calculation. Statistical software SPSS 17 is used for analyzed and calculation of data. The calculated mean value is put to various statistical analyses for testing the hypothesis of research. The statistical tools Chi-Square test, Regression, ANOVA, Rank Order, Co-efficient are used for calculation purpose.

Objective 1:   To study various determinants influence the buying behavior of Millennial on social media advertising

1. Effectiveness of social media tools on the consumer Behaviour –
   (i) Rank Order – Audience

Table 5.1: effectiveness of SNSs in terms of Audience

Rank	1	2	3	4	5	6	7	8	9	10	Total
Face book	31	19	15	20	25	33	81	106	66	120	3726
Twitter	20	19	28	45	74	75	102	62	54	37	3208
LinkedIn	29	30	25	47	63	54	63	2	52	61	3246

From the table 5.1 it was found that as an audience the millennial prefer most Face book and least preferred is prefer Twitter as the Social networking sites that have a large number of groups (networks) available for any demographics you are looking for; for instance group of teenagers, group of kids, youth, group of new moms, brides, sports fans, technology enthusiasts, entrepreneurs etc.

(ii) Rank Order – Targeting

Table 5.2: Effectiveness of SNSs in terms of targeting consumers

Rank	1	2	3	4	5	6	7	8	9	10	Total
Facebook	35	16	13	24	34	37	72	98	82	105	3670
Twitter	25	41	37	64	58	63	63	75	36	54	3047
LinkedIn	56	56	31	38	42	59	70	59	48	57	2941

From the above table it was found that as an audience the millennial prefer most Face book and least preferred is twitter as the Social networking site that targets the advertisements to specific group of audience.

2. Social Networking Sites having more followers due to acquaintances

Out of the total 514 valid respondents, a maximum of 83.3 % agreed that Face book more followers due to acquaintances and the minimum of 7.0 % respondents said that LinkedIn has more followers due to acquaintance.

Table 5.3: Effectiveness in terms of more followers

		Frequency	Percent	Valid Percent	Cumulative Percent
Valid	Face book	430	83.3	83.3	83.3
	Twitter	50	9.7	9.7	93.0
	LinkedIn	34	7.0	7.0	100.0
	Total	514	100.0	100.0	

3. Social Networking Sites having more unknown followers

Table 5.3: Effectiveness of SNSs in terms of more unknown followers

		Frequency	Percent	Valid Percent	Cumulative Percent
Valid	Face book	256	50.0	50.0	50.0
	Twitter	140	27.1	27.1	77.1
	LinkedIn	118	22.9	22.9	100.0
	Total	514	100.0	100.0	

Out of the total 514 respondents, a maximum percentage of 50.0 % said that face book has more unknown followers and minimum of 22.9 % said that LinkedIn has more unknown followers.

4. Use of SNS by IT Professional -

Table 5.4: Frequency of Millennial using internet on mobile or computer

		Freq.	Per. (%)	Valid %	Cu.%
Val.	Daily	385	74.9	74.9	74.9
	4-5 Day/Week	79	15.3	15.3	90.2
	2-3 Day/Week	27	5.2	5.2	95.4
	1 Day/Week	13	2.5	2.5	97.9
	Very Rare	8	1.5	1.5	99.3
	No.	4	.7	.7	100.0
	Total	514	100.0	100.0	

It can be observed from survey result that, from 514 IT professionals, 385 (74.9%) using internet on the daily basis, 79(15.3) using internet for social media platform 2 to 3 days per week and 2.5 % using internet one day per week whereas 8 using internet very rare and even 4 participants using no internet for SNS purpose.

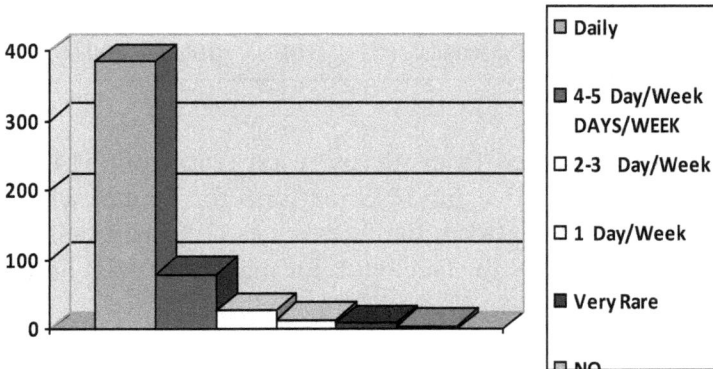

Figure 6.1: Millennial using internet on mobile or computer

5. Type of SNS - Face book

Table 5.5: Frequency of Millennial using Facebook SNS for social network

	Freq.	Per. (%)	Valid %	Cu.%
Y	411	81.2	81.2	81.2
N	103	18.8	18.8	99.8
Total	514	100.0	100.0	

It can be observed from survey result that, from 514 millennial IT professionals, 411 using SNS platform for Facebook whereas 101 not using the SNS platform for Facebook i.e. 81.2 % using SNS for FB and 18.6 not using SNS for face book for maintain social network.

6. Type of SNS – Twitter

Table 5.6: Frequency of millennial using twitters SNS for social network

		Freq.	Per. (%)	Valid %	Cu.%
V	Y	161	31.0	31.0	31.0
	N	355	69.0	69	100
	Total Participants	514	100.0	100.0	

It can be observed from survey result that, from 514 millennial IT professionals, 161 using SNS platform for Twitter whereas 355 not using the SNS platform for Twitter i.e. 31 % using SNS for FB and 69 not using SNS for face book for maintain social network.

7. Type of SNS - LinkedIn

Table 5.7: Frequency of Millennial using LinkedIn SNS for social network

		Freq.	Per. (%)	Valid %	Cu.%
Valid	Yes	132	26.6	18.9	18.9
	No	382	74.4	74.4	100.0
	Total	514	100.0	100.0	

It can be observed from survey result that, from 514 millennial IT professionals, 132 using SNS platform for LinkedIn whereas 382 not using the SNS platform for LinkedIn i.e. 26.6 % using SNS for FB and 74.4% not using SNS for LinkedIn for maintain social network.

8. Types of SNS- Others

Table 5.8: Frequency of Millennial using other SNS for social network

		Freq.	Per. (%)	Valid %	Cu.%
V	Y	29	5.7	5.7	5.7
	N	485	94.3	94.3	100
	Total Participants	514	100	100	

It can be observed from survey result that, from 514 millennial IT professionals, 29 using SNS platform for Other SNSs whereas 485 not using the SNS platform for Other SNSs i.e. 5.7% using SNS for FB and 94.3% not using SNS for Other SNSs for maintain social network.

9. Use frequency of SNS by IT Professional -
Table 5.9: Frequency of Millennial using SNS

		Freq.	Per. (%)	Valid %	Cu.%
Va	Daily	288	55.6	55.6	55.6
	4-5 D/w days/week	117	23.0	23.0	78.5
	2-3 D/w	39	7.8	7.8	86.3
	1 D/w	26	5.1	5.1	91.4
	very rare	19	3.6	3.6	95.0
	No	25	5.0	5.0	100.0
	total	514	100.0	100.0	

It can be observed from survey result that, from 514 IT
professionals, 288 (55.6%) using SNS platform on the daily basis,
117(23) using internet for social media platform 4 to 5 days per
week and 7.8 % using SNS platform 2 to 3 day per week whereas
19 very rare and 23 not using SNS platform very rare and even 4
participants not using SNS platform.

10. IT professional motivated for purchasing by SNS
Advertisement
Table 5.10: The number of interested to purchasing after
watch advertisement

		Freq.	Per. (%)	Valid %	Cu.%
V	y	480	93.3	93.3	93.3
	N	34	6.7	6.7	100.0
	Total	514	100.0	100.0	

It can be observed from survey result that, from 514 participants,
480 Millennial feel positive effect on advertisement and motivate to
purchase, 34 professionals not motivated by SNS advertisement.

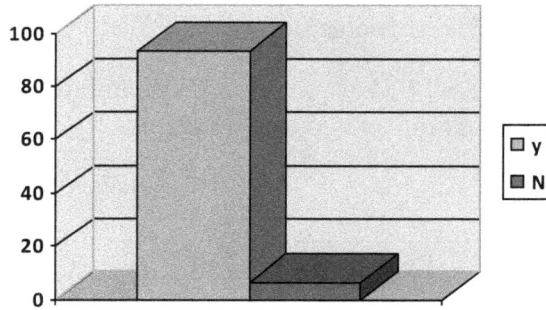

Figure 5.2: Millennial motivated for purchasing by SNS Advertisement

On the basis of percentage of 100% participants, 93.3% Millennial feel positive effect on advertisement and motivate to purchase, 6.7 % professionals not motivated by SNS advertisement.

11. Will you prefer to go to purchasing for consumer electronics without see the online review about price and product quality?

Table 6.11: Millennial prefer to go to purchasing without see the online review

		Freq.	Per. (%)	Valid %	Cu.%
V	Y	65	12.6	12.6	12.6
	N	449	87.4	87.4	100.0
	Total	514	100.0	100.0	

It can be observed from survey result that, from 514 participants, 65 Millennial have not concern about online review about price and product quality, 449 will check online review for price and quality check.

On the basis of percentage of 100% participants, 12.6% millennial have not concern about online review about price and product quality, 87.4% will check online review for price and quality check.

12. Will you prefer website of product only to go to purchasing for consumer electronics?

Table 5.11: Frequency of Millennial prefer website of product only to go to purchasing

		Freq.	Per. (%)	Valid %	Cu.%
V	Y	58	11.2	11.2	11.2
	N	456	88.7	88.7	100.0
	Total	514	100.0	100.0	

It can be observed from survey result that, from 514 participants, 58 prefer website of product only to go to purchasing for consumer electronics, 456 professionals will check by other source also.

On the basis of percentage of 100% participants, 11.2% prefer website of product only to go to purchasing for consumer electronics, 88.7% 456 professionals will check by other source also.

13. Will you prefer television and print media advertisement for purchasing?

Table 5.12: Frequency of prefers television and print media advertisement of product

		Freq.	Per. (%)	Valid %	Cu.%
V	Y	25	4.8	4.8	4.8
	N	489	95.1	95.1	100.0
	Total Participants	514	100.0	100.0	

It can be observed from survey result that, from 514 participants will prefer television and print media advertisement of product for purchasing of consumer electronics, 489 professionals denied that they prefer television and print media advertisement of product for purchasing of consumer electronics

On the basis of percentage of 100% participants, 4.8% will prefer television and print media advertisement of product for purchasing of consumer electronics, 95.1% professionals denied that they prefer television and print media advertisement of product for purchasing of consumer electronics

14. If you spend more time online, then chances of purchasing electronics items increased?

Table 5.13: Frequency of spending more time online

		Freq.	Per. (%)	Valid %	Cu.%
V	Y	496	96.4	96.4	3.5
	N	18	3.5	3.5	100.0
	Total Participants	514	100.0	100.0	

It can be observed from survey result that, from 514 participants, 496 Millennial Information technology professional agreed that If spend more time online, then chances of purchasing electronics items increased , 18 professionals denied that If spend more time online, then chances of purchasing electronics items increased

On the basis of percentage of 100% participants, 96.4% Millennial Information technology professional agreed that If spend more time online, then chances of purchasing electronics items increased, 3.5% professionals denied that they If spend more time online, then chances of purchasing electronics items increased

15. On which social networking advertisement you give more importance for purchasing of electronics items

Table 5.14: Frequency of SNS advertisement give more importance for purchasing

		Freq.	Per. (%)	Valid %	Cu.%
V	Facebook	147	28.5	28.5	28.5
	YouTube	115	22.3	22.3	50.8
	Twitter	136	26.4	26.4	77.3
	LinkedIn	87	16.9	16.9	94.2
	Other HOURS	29	5.8	5.8	100.0
	Total Participants	514	100.0	100.0	

It can be observed from survey result that, from 514 participants, 147 Millennial Information technology professional are giving first priority to Facebook, 115 Millennial Information technology professional are giving first priority to YouTube , 136 professionals agreed are giving first priority to twitter advertisement , 87 Information technology professional said that are giving first priority to LinkedIn and 29 IT professionals are giving first priority to other social networking sites. On the basis of percentage of 100% participants, 28.5% Millennial Information technology professional are giving first priority to Facebook, 22.3% professionals agreed are giving first priority to YouTube advertisement, 26.4% Information technology professional said that are giving first priority to twitter, 16.9% Information technology professional said that are giving first priority to LinkedIn and 5.8% IT professionals giving other SNS sites.

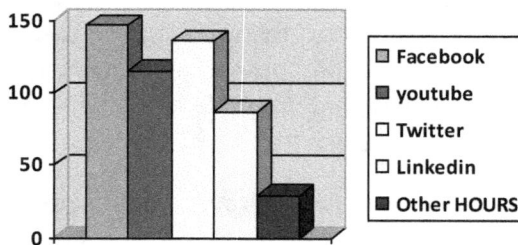

Figure 5.3: Frequently used Website for purchasing

16. At the time of final decision of purchasing how much time you spend on SNS

Table 5.15: Frequency of Millennial time spend on LinkedIn

		Freq.	Per. (%)	Valid %	Cu.%
V	15 min	138	26.8	26.8	26.8
	30 min	178	34.6	34.6	61.4
	1 hr.	95	18.4	18.4	79.8
	2 hr	57	11.1	11.1	90.9
	Greater than 2 hr. HOURS	46	9.1	9.1	100.0
	Total Participants	514	100.0	100.0	

It can be observed from survey result that, from 514 participants, 138 Millennial Information technology professional are spending 15 minute At the time of final decision of purchasing, 178 Millennial Information technology professional are spending 30 minute At the time of final decision of purchasing, 95 professionals agreed that they are spending At the time of final decision of purchasing, 57 Information technology professional said that spending At the time of final decision of purchasing and 46 IT professionals spending time more than 2hour.

On the basis of percentage of 100% participants, 26.8% Millennial Information technology professional are spending 15 minute At the time of final decision of purchasing, 34.6%Millennial Information technology professional are spending 30 minute At the time of final decision of purchasing, 18.4% professionals agreed that they are spending 1hour At the time of final decision of purchasing, 11.1% Information technology professional said that spending 1hour At the time of final decision of purchasing and 9.1% IT professionals spending time more than 2hour.

Objective 2:- To analyzed drivers, motives, reasons and factors affecting the buying behaviors of Millennial.

1. Relationship between online purchase behaviour with the factor of Social Media Advertisement i.e. "On which social network sites millennial find the product advertisement displayed attractive"

H0: There is no association between the factor i.e. "On which social network sites millennial find the product advertisement displayed attractive" with online purchase behaviour of millennial for consumer electronics.

H1: There is association between the factors i.e. "On which social network sites millennial find the product advertisement displayed attractive" with online purchase behaviour of millennial for consumer electronics

Chi-Square Tests

Table 5.16: Relationship between online purchase behavior

	Value	df	Asymp. Sig. (2-)
Pearson Chi-Square	25.900(a)	27	.524
Likelihood Ratio	26.993	27	.464
Linear-by-Linear	.016	1	.901
N of Valid Cases	514		

If X is a random variable having a $\chi2$ distribution with $v = 27$ degrees of freedom, then $p = \Pr[X \geq 25.000] = 0.5745$.

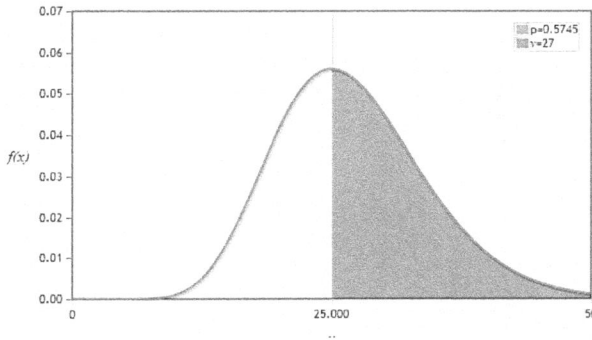

Figure 6.4:
Distribution chart for online purchase behaviour

From the above table, it is observed that at 5 % level of significance $p > \alpha$ (0.05), so the null hypothesis is accepted and alternative is rejected, so, we conclude that there is no association between the factor i.e. "On which social network sites millennial find the product advertisement displayed attractive" with online purchase behaviour of millennial for consumer electronics .

This means the factor i.e. "On which social network sites millennial find the product advertisement displayed attractive" with online purchase behaviour of millennial for consumer electronics are independent of each other. So, we can conclude that millennial feel that on social networking sites product advertisement displayed is not attractive and it does not affect their online purchase behaviour.

2. Relationship between online purchase behaviour with the factor of Social Media Advertisement i.e. "the millennial are having trust on the advertisements displayed on social networking sites" –

H0: There is no association between the factor i.e. "the millennial are having trust on the advertisements displayed on social networking sites" with online purchase behaviour of millennial or consumer electronics.

H1: There is association between the factor i.e. "the millennial are having trust on the advertisements displayed on social networking sites" with online purchase behaviour of millennial for consumer electronics.

Chi-Square Tests
Table 5.17: Relationship between online purchase behaviour with the trust factor of social media advertising

	Value	df	Asymp. Sig. (2-)
Pearson Chi-Square	34.725(a)	27	.146
Likelihood Ratio	37.779	27	.081
Linear-by-Linear	1.182	1	.277
N of Valid Cases	514		

If X is a random variable having a $\chi 2$ distribution with $v = 27$ degrees of freedom, then $p = \Pr[X \geq 34.725] = 0.1460$.

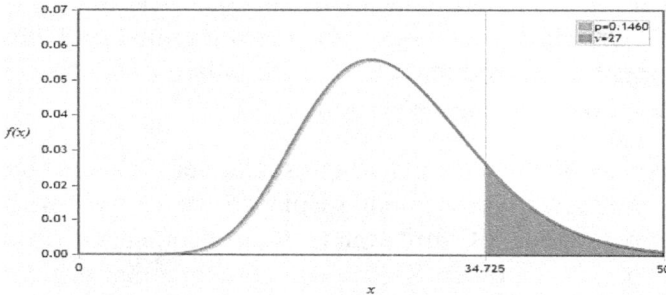

Figure 5.5: Distribution chart for online purchase behaviour with the trust factor

From the above table, it is observed at 5 % level of significance p > α (0.05), so the null hypothesis accepted and alternative is rejected, so, we conclude that there is no association between the factor i.e. "the millennial are having trust on the advertisements displayed on social networking sites" with online purchase behaviour of millennial for consumer electronics. This means the factor i.e. "the millennial are having trust on the advertisements displayed on social networking sites" with online purchase behaviour of millennial for consumer electronics because they are independent of each other for. So, we can conclude that millennial feel that on social networking sites are not trustworthy for the product advertisement display, which will not affect their online purchase behaviour.

3. How much your personal involvement in purchase decision?

Table 5.18: Frequency of Millennial involved in purchase decision

		Freq.	Per. (%)	Valid %	Cu.%
V	Absolutely	221	40.8	40.8	45.1
	moderate level	190	35.1	35.1	75.9
	Fair	56	10.3	10.3	86.2
	Less	47	13.8	13.8	100.0
	Total Participants	514	100.0	100.0	

It can be observed from survey result that, from 514 participants, 221 Millennial Information technology professional are absolutely involved in purchase decision , 190 professionals agreed that involved in purchase decision at moderate, 56 Information technology professional said that they personally absolutely involved in purchase decision at fair level and 47 IT professional agreed that , the they less involved in purchase decision

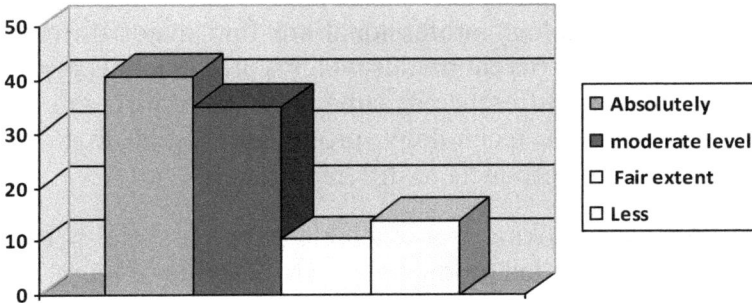

Figure 5.6: Millennial involved in purchase decision

On the basis of percentage of 100% participants, 40.8% Millennial Information technology professional are personally absolutely involved in purchase decision , 35.1% professionals agreed that involved in purchase decision at moderate , 10.3% Information technology professional said that they personally absolutely involved in purchase decision at fair level and 13.8%IT professional agreed that , the they less involved in purchase decision .

4. Are you found any difference in same product of different brands?

Table 5.19: Millennial find difference in same products of different brands

		Freq.	Per. (%)	Valid %	Cu.%
V	Major difference	264	51.36	51.36	51.36
	Medium	229	44.5	44.5	95.86
	No difference	21	4.14	4.14	100.0
	Total Participants	514	100.0	100.0	

It can be observed from survey result that, from 514 participants, 264 Millennial Information technology professional are find major difference in same products of different brands , 229 professionals agreed that they find medium difference in same products of different brands , 21 Information technology professional said that find no difference in same products of different brands

On the basis of percentage of 100% participants, 51.36% Millennial Information technology professional are find major difference in same products of different brands , 44.5% professionals agreed that they find medium difference in same products of different brands , 4.14% Information technology professional said that find no difference in same products of different brands.

5. Are you thinking that available price on social networking sites of branded product are high, accurate or low?

Table 5.20: Frequency of Millennial thinks about price

		Freq.	Per. (%)	Valid %	Cu.%
V	Higher	239	46.4	46.4	46.4
	Accurate	228	44.3	44.3	90.7
	Low	47	9.3	9.3	100.0
	Total	514	100.0	100.0	

It can be observed from survey result that, from 514 participants, 239 Millennial Information technology professional are think that available price on social networking sites of branded product are high, 228 professionals agreed that are think that available price on social networking sites of branded product are accurate, 47 Information technology professional said that are think that available price on social networking sites of branded product are low.

On the basis of percentage of 100% participants, 46.4% Millennial Information technology professional are think that available price on social networking sites of branded product are high, 44.3% professionals agreed that are think that available price on social networking sites of branded product are accurate, 9.3% Information technology professional said that are think that available price on social networking sites of branded product are low.

6. Are you agreed that purchase influenced by SNS advertisement is time consuming?

Table 5.21: Millennial agreed that purchase by SNS advertisement is time consuming

		Freq.	Per. (%)	Valid %	Cu.%
Valid	Many Times time consuming	137	26.6	26.6	26.6
	some time consuming	263	51.1	51.1	77.7
	Less time consuming	113	22.2	22.2	99.9
	4.00	1	.1	.1	100.0
	Total	514	100.0	100.0	

It can be observed from survey result that, from 514 participants, 137 Millennial Information technology professional are many time agreed that purchase decision influenced by SNS advertisement is time consuming, 263 professionals some time agreed that purchase decision influenced by SNS advertisement is time consuming, 113 Information technology professional said very less time agreed that purchase decision influenced by SNS advertisement is time consuming.

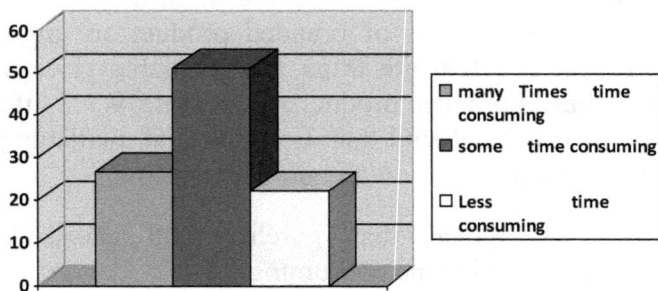

Figure 5.7: SMA influenced purchasing process timing

On the basis of percentage of 100% participants, 26.6% Millennial Information technology professional are many time agreed that purchase decision influenced by SNS advertisement is time consuming, 51.1%professionals some time agreed that purchase decision influenced by SNS advertisement is time consuming, 22.2%Information technology professional said very less time agreed that purchase decision influenced by SNS advertisement is time consuming.

7. Before purchasing electronic product, what type of product information you searched?

Table 5.22: Information search before purchasing

		Freq.	Per. (%)	Valid %	Cu.%
V	Broad search	142	27.6	27.6	27.6
	Moderate search	311	60.5	60.5	88.1

		48	9.3	9.3	97.4
	Minimum Search	48	9.3	9.3	97.4
	No search	12	2.6	2.6	99.9
	21.00	1	.1	.1	100.0
	Total	514	100.0	100.0	

It can be observed from survey result that, from 514 participants, 142 Millennial Information technology professional are searched broad information about product before purchasing electronic product ,311 professionals agreed that they searched moderate information about product before purchasing electronic product, 48 Information technology professional said that they searched minimum information about product before purchasing electronic product,12IT professional said they never searched information about product before purchasing electronic product.

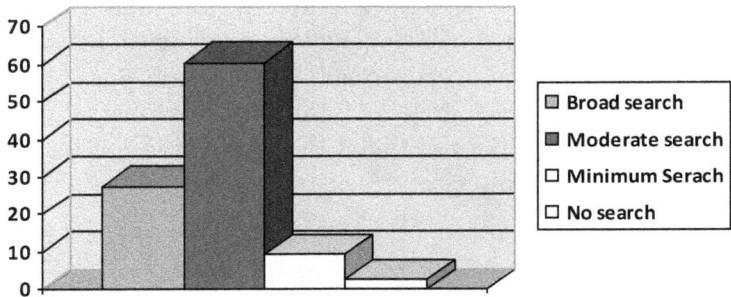

Figure 5.8: Information Search before purchasing

On the basis of percentage of 100% participants, 27.6% Millennial Information technology professional are searched broad information about product before purchasing electronic product ,60.5% professionals agreed that they searched moderate information about product before purchasing electronic product, 9.3% Information technology professional said that they searched minimum information about product before purchasing electronic product,2.6% IT professional said they never searched information about product before purchasing electronic product.

8. What is your frequency to visit advertisements of
electronics product on SNS?

Table 523: Frequency of Millennial visit advertisements
of product on SNS

		Freq.	Per. (%)	Valid %	Cu.%
V	Always	84	16.3	16.3	18.4
	Mostly	152	29.5	29.5	45.8
	Sometimes	198	38.5	38.5	84.3
	Occasionally	59	11.4	11.4	95.7
	Never	21	4.3	4.3	100.0
	Total	514	100.0	100.0	

It can be observed from survey result that, from 514 participants, 84Millennial Information technology professional are always visit advertisements of electronics product on SNS ,152 professionals agreed that they mostly visit advertisements of electronics product on SNS, 198 Information technology professional said that they are sometimes visit advertisements of electronics product on SNS,59 IT professional said they are Occasionally visit advertisements of electronics product on SNS and 21 never visit advertisement on social networking sites.

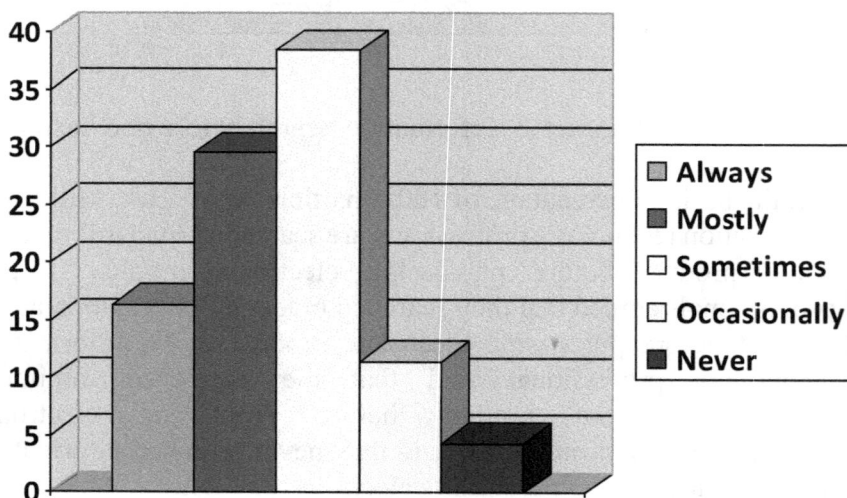

Figure 5.9: Millennial visit advertisements

On the basis of percentage of 100% participants, 16.3% Millennial Information technology professional are always visit advertisements of electronics product on SNS ,29.5% professionals agreed that they mostly visit advertisements of electronics product on SNS, 38.5% Information technology professional said that they are sometimes visit advertisements of electronics product on SNS,11.4%IT professional said they are Occasionally visit advertisements of electronics product on SNS and 4.3% never visit advertisement on social networking sites.

9. Before purchasing electronic product influenced by SNS advertisement, how much time you spend for information about product quality, uses, review?

Table 5.24: Millennial time spends for information about product quality, review?

		Freq.	Per. (%)	Valid %	Cu.%
V	More	106	20.6	20.6	20.6
	Adequate	236	45.9	45.9	66.5
	Some time	98	19.1	19.1	85.6
	Little	45	8.7	8.7	94.3
	None	29	5.7	5.7	100.0
	Total	514	100.0	100.0	

It can be observed from survey result that, from 514 participants, 243 Millennial Information technology professional are more time spend before purchasing decision for information about product quality, uses, review., ,185 professionals agreed that they adequate time spend before purchasing decision for information about product quality, uses, review, 47 Information technology professional said that they are more time spend some time before purchasing decision for information about product quality, uses, review,39 IT professional said they spend little time and 28 not spend any time for collection of information before purchasing.

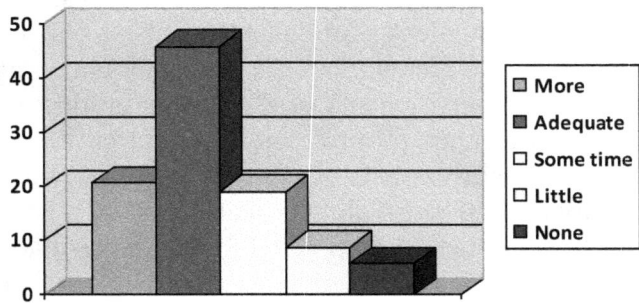

Figure 5.10: Spending time on SNS

On the basis of percentage of 100% participants, 243 Millennial Information technology professional are more time spend before purchasing decision for information about product quality, uses, review., ,185 professionals agreed that they adequate time spend before purchasing decision for information about product quality, uses, review, 47 Information technology professional said that they are more time spend some time before purchasing decision for information about product quality, uses, review,39 IT professional said they spend little time and 28 not spend any time for collection of information before purchasing.

10. What is the frequency of visit electronics shop before purchasing decision?

Table 5.25: Millennial visit electronics shop before purchasing decision

		Freq.	Per. (%)	Valid %	Cu.%
V	1-3	243	47.2	47.2	47.2
	3-5	185	35.9	35.9	83.1
	5-7	47	9.2	9.2	92.3
	More than 7	39	7.7	7.7	100.0
	Total	514	100.0	100.0	

It can be observed from survey result that, from 514 participants, 243 Millennial Information technology professional are 1 to 3 times visit electronics shop before purchasing decision, 185 professionals agreed that they visit 3 to 5 times electronics shop before purchasing decision, 47 Information technology professional said that they visit 5 to 7 times electronics shop before purchasing decision,39 IT professional said visit more than 7 times.

On the basis of percentage of 100% participants, 47.2% Millennial Information technology professional are 1 to 3 times visit electronics shop before purchasing decision, 35.9% professionals agreed that they visit 3 to 5 times electronics shop before purchasing decision, 9.2% Information technology professional said that they visit 5 to 7 times electronics shop before purchasing decision,7.7% IT professional said visit more than 7 times.

11. Before purchasing electronic product influenced by SNS advertisement, what attribute you consider?-? - (Product look)

Table 5.26: Millennial consider the look of product before purchasing product

		Freq.	Per. (%)	Valid %	Cu.%
V	Y	132	25.6	25.6	25.6
	N	382	74.4	74.4	100.0
	Total Participants	514	100.0	100.0	

It can be observed from survey result that, from 514 participants, 132 Millennial Information technology professional are consider the look of product before purchasing electronic product influenced by SNS advertisement, 382professionals not consider the look of product before purchasing electronic product influenced by SNS advertisement.

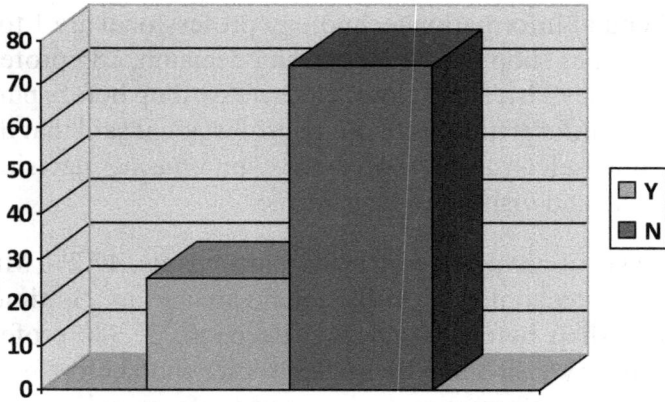

Figure 5.11: Millennial Considered product look

On the basis of percentage of 100% participants, 25.6% Millennial Information technology professional are consider the look of product before purchasing electronic product influenced by SNS advertisement., 74.4% professionals not consider the look of product before purchasing electronic product influenced by SNS advertisement.

12. Before purchasing electronic product influenced by SNS advertisement, what attribute you consider?-? -Function ability

Table 5.27: Frequency of Millennial consider the function ability before purchasing

		Freq.	Per. (%)	Valid %	Cu.%
V	Y	128	24.9	24.9	24.9
	N	386	75.1	75.1	100.0
	Total Participants	514	100.0	100.0	

It can be observed from survey result that, from 514 participants, 128 Millennial Information technology professional are consider the function ability before purchasing electronic product influenced by SNS advertisement, 386 professionals not consider the function ability before purchasing electronic product influenced by SNS advertisement.

On the basis of percentage of 100% participants, 24.9% Millennial Information technology professional are consider the function ability before purchasing electronic product influenced by SNS advertisement., 75.1% professionals not consider the function ability before purchasing electronic product influenced by SNS advertisement.

13. Before purchasing electronic product influenced by SNS advertisement, what attribute you consider? value.

Table 5.28: Millennial who consider the value before purchasing product

		Freq.	Per. (%)	Valid %	Cu.%
V	Y	246	47.8	47.8	46.0
	N	268	52.2	52.2	100.0
	Total Participants	514	100.0	100.0	

It can be observed from survey result that, from 514 participants, 246 Millennial Information technology professional are consider the value before purchasing electronic product influenced by SNS advertisement, 268 professionals not consider the value before purchasing electronic product influenced by SNS advertisement.

On the basis of percentage of 100% participants, 47.8% Millennial Information technology professional are consider the value before purchasing electronic product influenced by SNS advertisement, 52.2% professionals not consider the value before purchasing electronic product influenced by SNS advertisement.

14. Before purchasing electronic product influenced by SNS advertisement, what attribute you consider?-? -worth.

Table 5.29: Millennial consider the worth before purchasing electronic product

		Freq.	Per. (%)	Valid %	Cu.%
V	Y	284	55.2	55.2	55.2
	N	230	44.8	44.8	100.0
	Total Participants	514	100.0	100.0	

It can be observed from survey result that, from 514 participants, 284 Millennial Information technology professional are consider the worth before purchasing electronic product influenced by SNS advertisement., 230 professionals not consider the worth before purchasing electronic product influenced by SNS advertisement.

On the basis of percentage of 100% participants, 55.2% Millennial Information technology professional are consider the worth before purchasing electronic product influenced by SNS advertisement., 44.8% professionals not consider the worth before purchasing electronic product influenced by SNS advertisement.

15. Before purchasing electronic product influenced by SNS advertisement, what attribute you consider? - Reputation.

Table 5.30: Millennial consider the reputation before purchasing electronic product

		Freq.	Per. (%)	Valid %	Cu.%
V	Y	96	18.6	18.6	18.6
	N	418	81.4	81.4	100.0
	Total	514	100.0	100.0	

It can be observed from survey result that, from 514 participants, 96 Millennial Information technology professional are consider the reputation before purchasing electronic product influenced by SNS advertisement, 418 professionals not consider the reputation before purchasing electronic product influenced by SNS advertisement.

On the basis of percentage of 100% participants, 18.6% Millennial Information technology professional are consider the reputation before purchasing electronic product influenced by SNS advertisement, 81.4% professionals not consider the reputation before purchasing electronic product influenced by SNS advertisement.

16. Before purchasing electronic product influenced by SNS advertisement, what attribute you consider?-Relation with brand

Table 5.31: Millennial consider the relation with brands before purchasing

		Freq.	Per. (%)	Valid %	Cu.%
V	Y	57	11.2	11.2	11.2
	N	456	88.7	88.7	99.9
	4.00	1	.1	.1	100.0
	Total	514	100.0	100.0	

It can be observed from survey result that, from 514 participants , 57 Millennial Information technology professional are consider the relation with brands before purchasing electronic product influenced by SNS advertisement., 456 professionals not consider the relation with brands before purchasing electronic product influenced by SNS advertisement.

On the basis of percentage of 100% participants, 11.2%Millennial Information technology professional are consider the relation with brands before purchasing electronic product influenced by SNS advertisement., 88.7% professionals not consider the relation with brands before purchasing electronic product influenced by SNS advertisement.

17. Before purchasing electronic product influenced by SNS advertisement, what attribute you consider?-None

Table 5.32: Millennial who not consider any given attribute.

		Freq.	Per. (%)	Valid %	Cu.%
V	Y	23	4.4	4.4	4.4
	N	490	95.5	95.5	99.9
	7.00	1	.1	.1	100.0
	Total	514	100.0	100.0	

It can be observed from survey result that, from 514 participants , 23 Millennial Information technology professional are before purchasing electronic product influenced by SNS advertisement not consider any attribute, 490 professionals disagreed that before purchasing electronic product influenced by SNS advertisement not consider any attribute .

On the basis of percentage of 100% participants, 4.4% Millennial Information technology professional are before purchasing electronic product influenced by SNS advertisement not consider any attribute, 95.5% professionals disagreed that before purchasing electronic product influenced by SNS advertisement not consider any attribute .

18. Are you visiting shop before final decision of purchasing product for comparison of different available electronics product?

Table 5.33: Millennial who visit shop before final decision of purchasing product

		Freq.	Per. (%)	Valid %	Cu.%
V	Forever	182	35.4	35.4	35.4
	Frequently	178	34.6	34.6	70.0
	Sometimes	86	16.7	16.7	86.7

Rarely	43	8.2	8.2	94.9
No	25	5.1	5.1	100.0
Total	514	100.0	100.0	

It can be observed from survey result that, from 514 participants , 182 Millennial Information technology professional, forever visit shop before final decision of purchasing product for comparison of different available electronics product , 178 professionals frequently visit shop before final decision of purchasing product for comparison of different available electronics product, 86 Information technology professional said that they sometime visit shop before final decision of purchasing product for comparison of different available electronics product,43 IT professional said that they are rarely visit the shop, whereas 25 said that they don't visit shop before final decision of purchasing product for comparison of different available electronics product.

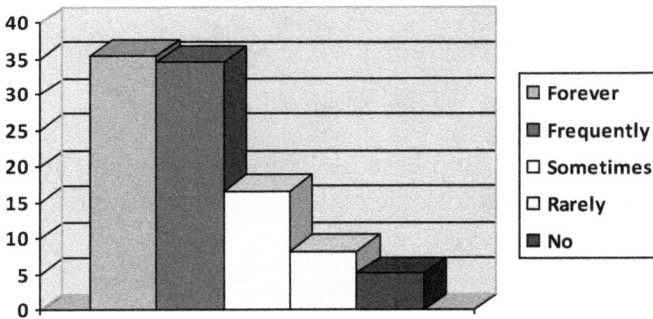

Figure 5.12: Millennial visit shop before final decision of purchasing

On the basis of percentage of 100% participants , 35.4% Millennial Information technology professional, forever visit shop before final decision of purchasing product for comparison of different available electronics product , 34.6% professionals frequently visit shop before final decision of purchasing product for comparison of different available electronics product, 16.7%Information technology professional said that they sometime visit shop before final decision of purchasing product for comparison of different available electronics product,8.2% IT professional said that they are rarely visit the shop, whereas 5.1% said that they don't visit shop before final decision of purchasing product for comparison of different available electronics product.

Objective 3 -To study theme and appeal which influence the buying behavior of Millennial

1. Relationship between consumer buying behaviour with the factor of Social Media Advertisement i.e. "Social network site the advertisements displayed appeal you" –

H0: There is no association between the factor i.e. "Social network site the advertisements displayed appeal you" with Consumer buying behavior of millennial for consumer electronics H1a: There is association between the factor i.e. "Social network site the advertisements displayed appeal you" with Consumer buying behaviour of millennial for consumer electronics

Chi-Square Tests

Table 5.34: Relationship between consumers buying behaviour with the appealing factor of social media advertisement towards advertisements displayed on SNS

	Value	Df	Asymp. Sig. (2)
Pearson Chi-Square	39.429(a)	6	.000
Likelihood Ratio	34.623	6	.000
Linear-by-LiLinear	22.184	1	.000
N of Valid Cases	514		

If X is a random variable having a $\chi 2$ distribution with $v = 6$ degrees of freedom, then $p = Pr[X \geq 39.429] = 0.0000$

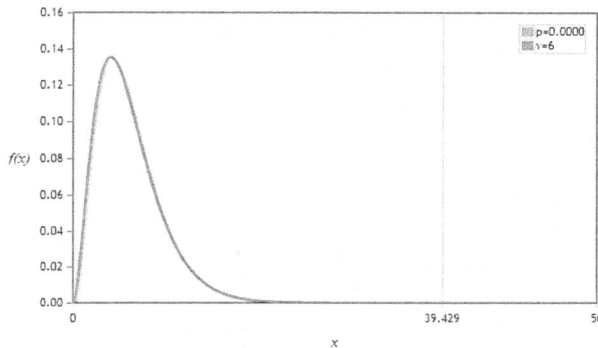

Figure 5.13: Distribution chart for buying behaviour with the appealing factor

From the above table, it is observed that at 5 % level of significance $p < \alpha$ (0.05), so the null hypothesis is rejected and alternative is accepted. Therefore, we can conclude that there is association between the factors i.e. "Social network site the advertisements displayed appeal you" with Consumer buying behaviour of millennial for consumer electronics. This means the factor i.e. "Social network site the advertisements displayed appeal you" Consumer buying behaviour of millennial for consumer electronics are dependent of each other. Further to check how much association exists between them we will use the Contingency Coefficient Statistics.

Symmetric Measures

Table 5.35: Symmetric Measures to determine how much relationship exists in between consumer buying behaviour and the appealing factor of social media advertising towards advertisements displayed on SNS

		Value	Approx. Sig.
Nominal by Nominal	Contingency Coef	.766	.000
N of Valid Cases		514	

107

From the above table 6.35, it is observed that there is a very strong positive opinion that advertisement displayed on social media appeals millennial to a great extent for buying electronics products and it affects consumer buying behaviour by 76.6 %.

2.   Relationship between consumer buying behaviour with the factor of Social Media Advertisement i.e. "on social networking sites the visuals and slogans of the advertisements displayed are memorable" –

H0: There is no association between the factor i.e. "on social networking sites the visuals and slogans of the advertisements displayed are memorable" with Consumer buying behaviour of millennial for consumer electronics .

H1 : There is association between the factor i.e. "on social networking sites the visuals and slogans of the advertisements displayed are memorable" with Consumer buying behaviour of millennial for consumer electronics .

Chi-Square Tests
Table 5.36: Relationship between consumer buying behaviour with the factor of memorable visuals and slogans of the advertisements

	Value	Df	Asymp. Sig. (2-sided)
Pearson Chi-Square	36.721(a)	26	.566
Likelihood Ratio	38.522	26	.044
Linear –by Linear	14.979	1	.444
No. of valid case	514		

If X is a random variable having a $\chi 2$ distribution with $v = 26$ degrees of freedom, then $p = \Pr[X \geq 36.721] = 0.0792$.

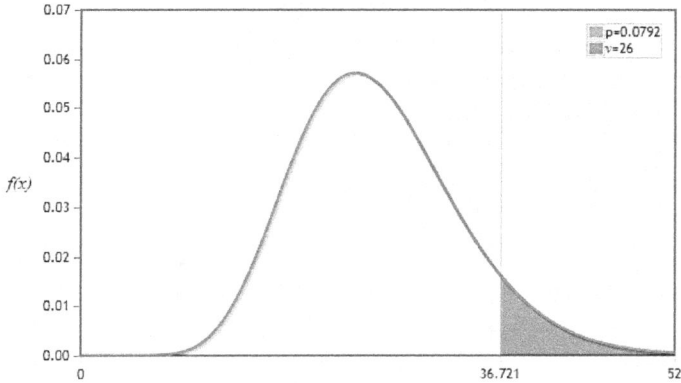

Figure 5.14: Distribution chart for factor of memorable visuals and slogans

From the above table, it is observed that at 5 % level of significance p > α (0.05), so the null hypothesis accepted and alternative is rejected, therefore, we conclude that there is no association between the factor i.e. "on Social networking sites the visuals and slogans of the advertisements displayed are memorable" with Consumer buying behaviour of millennial for consumer electronics . This means the factor i.e. on social networking sites the visuals and slogans of the advertisements displayed are memorable" with Consumer buying behaviour of millennial for consumer electronics are independent of each other. So, we can conclude that the visuals and slogans of the advertisement displayed on social media sites are not memorable for millennial while buying electronics products and it will not affect consumer buying behaviour.

2. Relationship between consumer buying behaviour with the factor of Social Media Advertisement i.e. "On which social network sites millennial find the product advertisement displayed attractive" –

H0 : There is no association between the factor i.e. "On which social network sites millennial find the product advertisement displayed attractive" with Consumer buying behaviour of millennial for consumer electronics .

H1 : There is no association between the factor i.e. "On which social network sites millennial find the product advertisement displayed attractive" with Consumer buying behaviour of millennial for consumer electronics .

Chi-Square Tests

Table 5.37: Relationship between consumer buying behaviour with the attractive factor of the advertisements displayed on SNS .

	Value	Df	Asymp. Sig.
Pearson Chi-Square	39.452(a)	28	.811
Likelihood Ratio	36.467	28	.066
Linear-by-Linear	25.847	1	.455
N of Valid Cases	514		

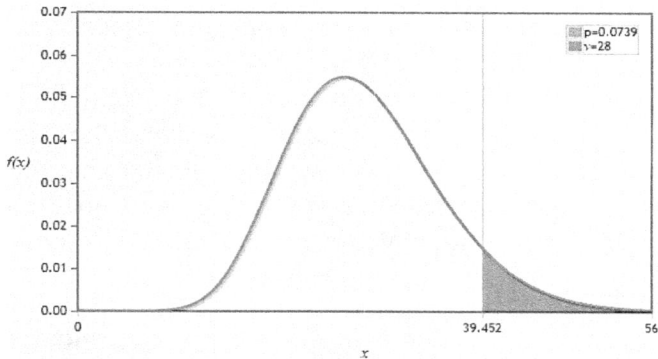

Figure 5.15: Distribution chart for attractive factor of the advertisements

From the above table, it is observed that at 5 % level of significance $p > \alpha$ (0.05), so the null hypothesis is accepted and alternative is rejected, so, we conclude that there is no association between the factor i.e. "On which social network sites millennial find the product advertisement displayed attractive" with Consumer buying behaviour of millennial for consumer electronics . This means the factor i.e. "On which social network sites millennial find the product advertisement displayed attractive" and Consumer buying behaviour of millennial for consumer electronics are independent of each other. So, we can conclude that millennial feel that on social networking sites product advertisement displayed is not attractive and it will not affect their consumer buying behaviour.

3. Relationship between consumer buying behaviour with the factor of Social Media Advertisement i.e. "the millennial are having trust on the advertisements displayed on social networking sites" –

H0: There is no association between the factor i.e. "the millennial are having trust on the advertisements displayed on social networking sites" with Consumer buying behaviour of millennial for consumer electronics.

H1: There is association between the factor i.e. "the millennial are having trust on the advertisements displayed on social networking sites" with Consumer buying behaviour of millennial for consumer electronics

Chi-Square Tests

Table 5.38: Relationship between consumers buying behaviour with the trustworthiness factor of the advertisements displayed on SNS.

	Value	Df	Asymp.
Pearson Chi-Square	26.061(a)	6	.089
Likelihood Ratio	26.905	6	.055
Linear-by-Linear Association	20.660	1	.333
N of Valid Cases	514		

If X is a random variable having a $\chi 2$ distribution with $v = 18$ degrees of freedom, then $p = \Pr[X \geq 26.061] = 0.0984$.

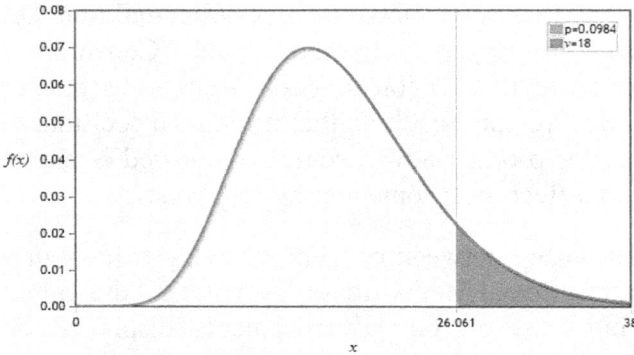

Figure 5.16: Distribution chart for trustworthiness factor

From the above table, it is observed that at 5 % level of significance p > α (0.05), so the null hypothesis is accepted and alternative is rejected, therefore, we conclude that there is no association between the factor i.e. "the millennial are having trust on the advertisements displayed on social networking sites" with Consumer buying behaviour of millennial for consumer electronics . This means the factor i.e. "the millennial are having trust on the advertisements displayed on social networking sites" with Consumer buying behaviour of millennial for consumer electronics are independent of each other. So, we can conclude that millennial feel that the product advertisement displayed on social networking sites are not trustworthy and it will not affect their consumer buying behaviour.

4. Relationship between online purchase behavior with the factor of Social Media Advertisement i.e. "Social network site the advertisements displayed appeal you" –

H0: There is no association between the factors i.e. "On social network sites the advertisements displayed appeal you" with online purchase behavior of millennial for consumer electronics.
H1 : There is association between the factor i.e. "On social network sites the advertisements displayed appeal you" with online purchase behavior of millennial for consumer electronics.

Chi-Square Tests

Table 5.39: Relationship between online purchase behaviour with the appealing factor of social media advertisements displayed on SNS .

	Value	Df	Asymp. Sig. (2-sided)
Pearson Chi-Square	31.469(a)	27	.252
Likelihood Ratio	32.253	27	.223
Linear-by-Linear	5.285	1	.022
No. of valid case	514		

If X is a random variable having a χ^2 distribution with $v = 27$ degrees of freedom, then $p = \Pr[X \geq 31.469] = 0.2523$.

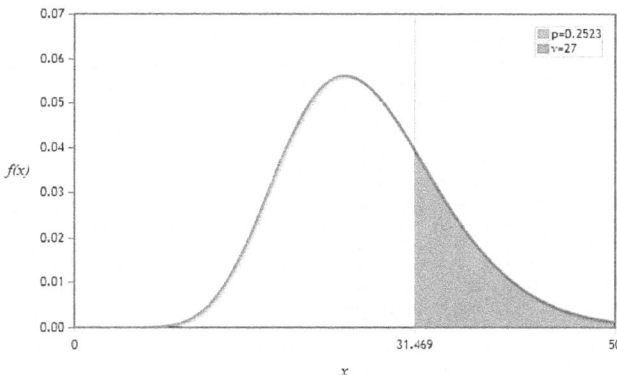

Figure 5.17: Distribution chart for appealing factor

From the above table, it is observed that at 5 % level of significance $p > \alpha$ (0.05), so the null hypothesis is accepted and alternative is rejected, so, we conclude that there is no association between the factor i.e. "On social network sites the advertisements displayed appeal you" with online purchase behaviour of millennial for consumer electronics . This means the factor i.e. "On social network sites the advertisements displayed appeal you" with online purchase behaviour of millennial for consumer electronics are independent of each other. So, we can conclude that the social network sites the advertisements are not appealing the millennial. So, it will not affect the online purchase behaviour of millennial.

5. Relationship between online purchase behaviour with the factor of Social Media Advertisement i.e. "on social networking sites the visuals and slogans of the advertisements displayed are memorable" –

H0: There is no association between the factor i.e. "on social networking sites the visuals and slogans of the advertisements displayed are memorable" with online purchase behaviour of millennial for consumer electronics
H1: There is association between the factor i.e. "on social networking sites the visuals and slogans of the advertisements displayed are memorable" with online purchase behaviour of millennial for consumer electronics

Chi-Square Tests
Table 5.40: Relationship between online purchase behaviour with the factor of social media advertising i.e. memorable visuals and slogans of the advertisements displayed on SNS .

	Value	Df	Asymp. Sig. (2-)
Pearson Chi-Square	28.851(a)	36	.796
Likelihood Ratio	29.508	36	.769
Linear-by-Linear	2.927	1	.087
No. of valid case	514		

If X is a random variable having a $\chi2$ distribution with $v = 36$ degrees of freedom, then $p = \Pr[X \geq 28.851] = 0.7955$.

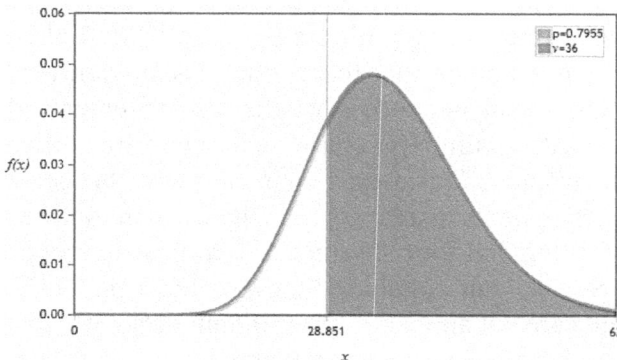

114

Figure 5.18: Distribution chart for visual and slogan

From the above table, it is observed that at 5 % level of significance p > α (0.05), so the null hypothesis is accepted and alternative is rejected, so, we conclude that there is no association between the factor i.e. "on Social networking sites the visuals and slogans of the advertisements displayed are memorable" with online purchase behaviour of millennial for consumer electronics. This means the factor i.e. on social networking sites the visuals and slogans of the advertisements displayed are memorable" with online purchase behaviour of millennial for consumer electronics are independent of each other. So, we can conclude that the visuals and slogans of the advertisement displayed on social media sites are not memorable for millennial while buying electronics products and it does not affect the online purchase behaviour.

6.   Relationship between online purchase behaviour with the factor of Social Media Advertisement i.e. "On which social network sites millennial find the product advertisement displayed attractive"

H_0: There is no association between the factor i.e. "On which social network sites millennial find the product advertisement displayed attractive" with online purchase behaviour of millennial for consumer electronics .

H_1 : There is association between the factor i.e. "On which social network sites millennial find the product advertisement displayed attractive" with online purchase behaviour of millennial for consumer electronics

Chi-Square Tests

Table 5.40:   Relationship between online purchase behaviour with the attractive factor of social media advertising.

	Value	df	Asymp. Sig. (2-sided)
Pearson Chi-Square	25.900(a)	27	.524

Likelihood Ratio	26.993	27	.464
Linear-by-Linear	.016	1	.901
N of Valid Cases	514		

If X is a random variable having a $\chi 2$ distribution with $v = 27$ degrees of freedom, then $p = \Pr[X \geq 25.900] = 0.5242$.

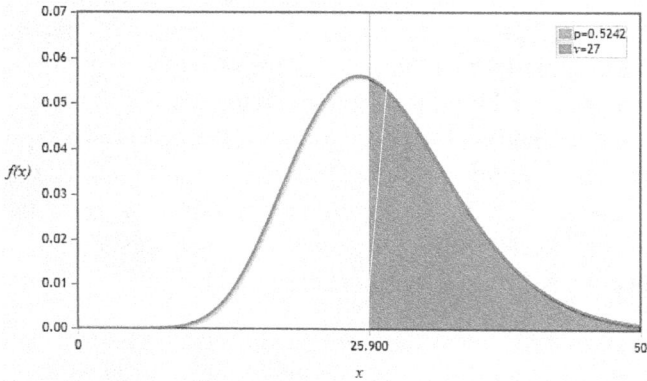

Figure 5.19: Distribution chart for attractive factor

From the above table, it is observed that at 5 % level of significance $p > \alpha$ (0.05), so the null hypothesis is accepted and alternative is rejected, so, we conclude that there is no association between the factor i.e. "On which social network sites millennial find the product advertisement displayed attractive" with online purchase behaviour of millennial for consumer electronics . This means the factor i.e. "On which social network sites millennial find the product advertisement displayed attractive" with online purchase behaviour of millennial for consumer electronics are independent of each other. So, we can conclude that millennial feel that on social networking sites product advertisement displayed is not attractive and it does not affect their online purchase behaviour.

7. Relationship between online purchase behaviour with the factor of Social Media Advertisement i.e. "the millennial are having trust on the advertisements displayed on social networking sites" –

116

H_0: There is no association between the factor i.e. "the millennialare having trust on the advertisements displayed on social networking sites" with online purchase behaviour of millennial or consumer electronics.

H1: There is association between the factor i.e. "the millennial are having trust on the advertisements displayed on social networking sites" with online purchase behaviour of millennial for consumer electronics.

Chi-Square Tests

Table 5.41: Relationship between online purchase behaviour with the trust factor of social media advertising

	Value	df	Asymp. Sig. (2-sided)
Pearson Chi-Square	34.725(a)	27	.146
Likelihood Ratio	37.779	27	.081
Linear-by-Linear	1.182	1	.277
N of Valid Cases	514		

If X is a random variable having a $\chi 2$ distribution with $v = 27$ degrees of freedom, then $p = \Pr[X \geq 34.725] = 0.1460$.

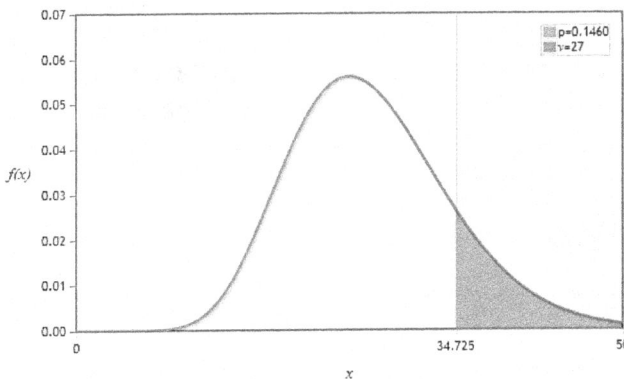

Figure 6.20: Frequently used Website for purchasing

Figure 5.20: Distribution chart for trust factor

From the above table, it is observed at 5 % level of significance p > α (0.05), so the null hypothesis accepted and alternative is rejected, so, we conclude that there is no association between the factor i.e. "the millennial are having trust on the advertisements displayed on social networking sites" with online purchase behaviour of millennial for consumer electronics. This means the factor i.e. "the millennial are having trust on the advertisements displayed on social networking sites" with online purchase behaviour of millennial for consumer electronics because they are independent of each other for. So, we can conclude that millennial feel that on social networking sites are not trustworthy for the product advertisement display, which will not affect their online purchase behaviour.

8. Relationship between complex buying behaviour with the factor of SMA i.e. "Social network site the advertisements displayed appeal you" –

H_0: There is no association between the factor i.e. "Social network site the advertisements displayed appeal you" with Complex buying behaviour of millennial for consumer electronics.

H_1: There is association between the factor i.e. "Social network site the advertisements displayed appeal you" with Complex buying behaviour of millennial for consumer electronics

Chi-Square Tests

Table 5.42: Relationship between complex buying behaviour with the appealing factor of social media advertising

	Value	df	Asymp. Sig. (2-sided)
Pearson Chi-Square	73.963(a)	36	.213
Likelihood Ratio	71.617	36	.112
Linear-by-Linear	33.921	1	.023
N of Valid Cases	514		

If X is a random variable having a $\chi2$ distribution with $v = 36$ degrees of freedom, then $p = \Pr[X \geq 73.963] = 0.2002$

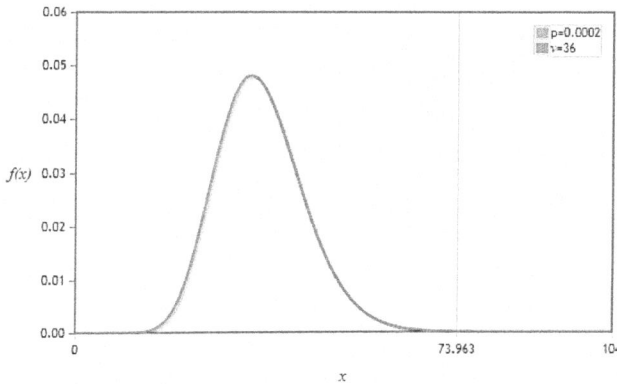

Figure 5.21: Distribution chart for appealing factor in complex behaviour

From the above table, it is observed that at 5 % level of significance p < α (0.05), so the null hypothesis is rejected and alternative is accepted, so, we conclude that there is association between the factor i.e. "Social network site the advertisements displayed appeal you" with Complex buying behaviour of millennial for consumer electronics.

This means the factor i.e. "Social network site the advertisements displayed appeal you" with Complex buying behaviour of millennial for consumer electronics are independent of each other. So, we can conclude that the advertisements displayed on social media sites appeal millennial while buying electronics products which will not affect Complex buying behaviour.

9. Relationship between Complex buying behaviour with the factor of Social Media Advertisement i.e. "social networking sites the visuals and slogans of the advertisements displayed are memorable" –

H_0: There is no association between the factor i.e. "social networking sites the visuals and slogans of the advertisements displayed are memorable" with Complex buying behaviour of millennial for consumer electronics

H_1: There is association between the factor i.e. "social networking sites the visuals and slogans of the advertisements displayed are memorable" with Complex buying behaviour of millennial for consumer electronics

Chi-Square Tests

Table 5.43: Relationship between complex buying behaviour with the memorable visuals and slogans factor of social media advertising

	Value	Df	Asymp. Sig. (2-sided)
Pearson Chi-Square	95.886(a)	48	.000
Likelihood Ratio	93.643	48	.000
Linear-by-Linear	31.763	1	.000
N of Valid Cases	514		

If X is a random variable having a $\chi 2$ distribution with $v = 48$ degrees of freedom, then $p = \Pr[X \geq 95.886] = 0.0000$.

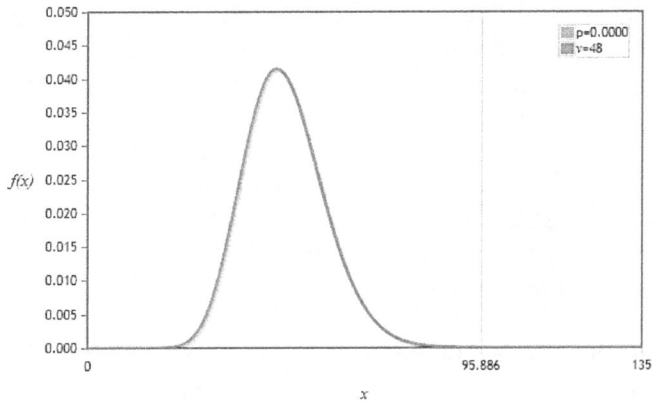

Figure 5.22: Distribution chart for memorable visual in complex behaviour

From the above table, it is observed that at 5 % level of significance $p < \alpha$ (0.05), so the null hypothesis is rejected and alternative is accepted, so, we conclude that there is association between the factor i.e. "Social networking sites the visuals and slogans of the advertisements displayed are memorable" with Complex buying behaviour of millennial for consumer electronics . This means the factor i.e. "social networking sites the visuals and slogans of the advertisements displayed are memorable" with Complex buying behaviour of millennial for consumer electronics are dependent of each other. Further to check how much association is existing, the Phi & Cramer's V Statistics is used.

Symmetric Measures

Table 6.44: Symmetric measures to determine how much relationship exists between complex buying behaviour and the memorable visuals and slogans factor

		Value	Approx. Sig.
Nominal by Nominal	Phi & Cramer's V	.731	.000
N of Valid Cases		514	

From the above table, it is observed that the visuals and slogans of the advertisements displayed are memorable according to the opinion of the millennial, which will affect Complex buying behaviour by 73.1 %.

10. Relationship between Complex buying behaviour with the factor of Social Media Advertisement i.e. "On which social network sites millennial find the product advertisement displayed attractive"

H_0: There is no association between the factors i.e. "On which social network sites millennial find the product advertisement displayed attractive" with Complex buying behaviour of millennial

H_1: There is association between the factors i.e. "On which social network sites millennial find the product advertisement displayed attractive" with Complex buying behaviour of millennial for consumer electronics

Chi-Square Tests

Table 5.45: Relationship between complex buying behaviour with the attractive factor of social media advertising

	Value	df	Asymp. Sig. (2-sided)
Pearson Chi-Square	19.452(a)	6	.788
Likelihood Ratio	26.467	6	.121
Linear-by-Linear	35.847	1	.344
N of Valid Cases	514		

If X is a random variable having a $\chi 2$ distribution with $v = 6$ degrees of freedom, then $p = \Pr[X \geq 19.452] = 0.0035$.

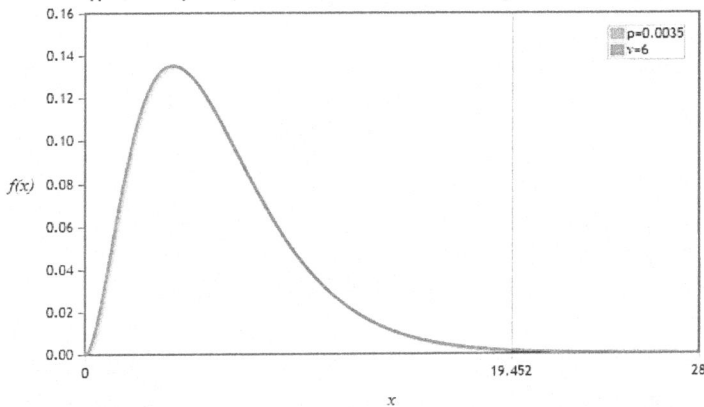

Figure 5.23: Distribution chart for attractive factor in complex

From the above table, it is observed that at 5 % level of significance $p < \alpha$ (0.05), so the null hypothesis is rejected and alternative is accepted, so, we conclude that there is association between the factor i.e. "On which social network sites millennial find the product advertisement displayed attractive" with Complex buying behaviour of millennial for consumer electronics . This means the factor i.e. "On which social network sites millennial find the product advertisement displayed attractive" with Complex buying behaviour of millennial for consumer electronics are independent of each other. So, we can conclude that millennial feel that on social networking sites product advertisement displayed is attractive which will affect their Complex buying behaviour.

11. Are you agreed that sometimes you have no plan for purchasing electronic products, at the time of login on SNS websites?

Table 5.46: Frequency of Millennial who agreed that sometimes no plan for purchasing electronic products, at the time of login on SNS websites

		Freq.	Per. (%)	Valid %	Cu.%
V	Str. Agreed	101	19.6	19.6	19.6
	Agreed	287	55.8	55.8	75.4
	Disagreed	102	19.8	19.8	95.2

123

		24	4.8	4.8	100.0
	Str. Disagreed				
	Total Participants	514	100.0	100.0	

It can be observed from survey result table no. 6.46 that, from 514 participants , 101 Millennial Information technology professional are strongly agreed that sometimes no plan for purchasing electronic products, at the time of login on SNS websites, 287 professionals agreed that sometimes no plan for purchasing electronic products, at the time of login on SNS websites, 102 Information technology professional said that they are not satisfied and disagreed that sometimes no plan for purchasing electronic products, at the time of login on SNS websites,24 IT professional said that they are strongly disagreed that s sometimes no plan for purchasing electronic products, at the time of login on SNS websites.

On the basis of percentage of 100% participants , 19.6% Millennial Information technology professional are strongly agreed that sometimes no plan for purchasing electronic products, at the time of login on SNS websites, 55.8% professionals agreed that sometimes no plan for purchasing electronic products, at the time of login on SNS websites, 19.8% Information technology professional said that they are not satisfied and disagreed that sometimes no plan for purchasing electronic products, at the time of login on SNS websites,4.8% IT professional said that they are strongly disagreed that s sometimes no plan for purchasing electronic products, at the time of login on SNS websites.

12. Are you agreed that sometimes purchasing done only due to SNS displayed lucrative Advertisement?

Table 5.47: Millennial who agreed that sometimes purchasing done only due to SNS displayed lucrative Advertisement

		Freq.	Per. (%)	Valid %	Cu.%
V	Str. Agreed	139	27.1	27.1	27.1
	Agreed	271	52.8	52.8	79.9

	Disagreed	91	17.8	17.8	97.7
	Str. Disagreed	13	2.2	2.2	99.9
	22.00	1	.1	.1	100.0
	Total Participants	514	100.0	100.0	

It can be observed from survey result that, from 514 participants , 139 Millennial Information technology professional are strongly agreed that sometimes purchasing done only due to SNS displayed lucrative Advertisement, 271 professionals agreed that sometimes purchasing done only due to SNS displayed lucrative Advertisement, 91 Information technology professional said that they are not satisfied and disagreed that sometimes purchasing done only due to displayed lucrative Advertisement,13 IT professional said that they are strongly disagreed that sometimes purchasing done only due to displayed lucrative Advertisement.

On the basis of percentage of 100% participants, 27.1%Millennial Information technology professional are strongly agreed that sometimes purchasing done only due to SNS displayed lucrative Advertisement, 52.8% professionals agreed that sometimes purchasing done only due to SNS displayed lucrative Advertisement, 17.8% Information technology professional said that they are not satisfied and disagreed that sometimes purchasing done only due to displayed lucrative Advertisement,2.2% IT professional said that they are strongly disagreed that sometimes purchasing done only due to displayed lucrative Advertisement.

Are you agreed that sometimes you purchased product because on SNS Advertisement displayed more attractive offer but not available in shops

Table 5.48: Frequency of Millennial IT professional who agreed that sometimes purchased product because on SNS Advertisement displayed more attractive offer not available in shops

		Freq.	Per. (%)	Valid %	Cu.%
V	Str. Agreed	107	20.8	20.8	20.8
	Agreed	299	58.1	58.1	78.9

125

	Disagreed	84	16.3	16.3	95.2
	Str. Disagreed	24	4.6	4.6	100.0
	Total	514	100.0	100.0	

Out of 514 respondents, 105 IT Professional strongly agree that at times they buy a product just because they find the discount scheme displayed in the advertisement on the social networking site interesting and not available in the retail stores, 301 IT Professional agree, 86 IT Professional disagree and 22 IT Professional strongly disagree that at times they buy a product just because they find the discount scheme displayed in the advertisement on the social networking site interesting and not available in the retail stores. Out of 100% respondents, 20.0% IT Professional strongly agree that at times they buy a product just because they find the discount scheme displayed in the advertisement on the social networking site interesting and not available in the retail stores, 58.7% IT Professional agree, 16.9% IT Professional disagree and 4.4% IT Professional strongly disagree that at times they buy a product just because they find the discount scheme displayed in the advertisement on the social networking site interesting and not available in the retail stores.

13. Analysis of available popular websites (Like FB, Twitter, LinkedIn) on SNS platform for different parameter -On SNS, in which website you like most?

Table 5.49: Frequency of Millennial according to personal liking of SNS websites

		Freq.	Per. (%)	Valid %	Cu.%
Valid	FB	434	84.4	84.4	84.4
	TWT	52	10.2	10.2	94.6
	LIKDN	28	4.4	4.4	100.0
	Total Participants	514	100.0	100.0	

It can be observed from survey result that, from 514 participants , 434 Millennial Information technology professional are like face book, 52 professionals said that they are like twitter, 28 Information technology professional said that they like LinkedIn, when they visiting SNS websites. On the basis of percentage of 100% participants , 84.4% Millennial Information technology professional are like face book, 10.2% professionals said that they are like twitter, 4.4 % Information technology professional said that they like LinkedIn, when they visiting SNS websites.

14. On SNS, in which website useful?
Table 5.50: Frequency of Millennial according to usefulness of SNS website

		Freq.	Per. (%)	Valid %	Cu.%
V	FB	329	64.0	64.0	64.0
	TWT	108	21.1	21.1	85.1
	LIKDN	77	14.9	14.9	100.0
	Total Participants	514	100.0	100.0	

It can be observed from survey result that, from 514 participants , 329 Millennial Information technology professional are normally use face book, 108 professionals said that they are normally use on twitter, 77 Information technology professional said that they normally use LinkedIn, when they visiting SNS websites.

On the basis of percentage of 100% participants , 64% Millennial Information technology professional are normally use face book, 21.1% professionals said that they are normally use on twitter, 14.9 % Information technology professional said that they normally use LinkedIn, when they visiting SNS websites.

15. On SNS, in which website normally you use?

Table 5.51: Frequency of Millennial according to use of SNS websites

		Freq.	Per. (%)	Valid %	Cu.%
Valid	FB	365	71.01	71.01	71.01
	TWT	81	15.6	15.6	86.3
	LIKDN	67	13.6	13.6	99.9
	11.00	1	.1	.1	100.0
	Total	514	100.0	100.0	

It can be observed from survey result that, from 514 participants , 365 Millennial Information technology professional are normally use face book, 81 professionals said that they are normally use on twitter, 67 Information technology professional said that they normally use LinkedIn, when they visiting SNS websites.

On the basis of percentage of 100% participants , 71.01% Millennial Information technology professional are normally use face book, 15.6% professionals said that they are normally use on twitter, 13.6% Information technology professional said that they normally use LinkedIn, when they visiting SNS websites.

16. On SNS, in which website you feel easy to use?

Table 5.52: Frequency of Millennial according to easiness of SNS websites

		Freq.	Per. (%)	Valid %	Cu.%
V	FB	378	73.5	73.5	73.5
	TWT	86	16.7	16.7	90.2
	LIKDN	49	9.7	9.7	99.9
	4.00	1	.1	.1	100.0
	Total Participants	514	100.0	100.0	

It can be observed from survey result that, from 514 participants , 378 Millennial Information technology professional are feel face book easy to use, 86 professionals said that they are feel easy on twitter, 49 Information technology professional said that they see more easiness on LinkedIn, when they visiting SNS websites.

On the basis of percentage of 100% participants , 73.5% Millennial Information technology professional are feel face book easy to use, 16.7% professionals said that they are feel easy on twitter, 9.7% Information technology professional said that they see more easiness on LinkedIn, when they visiting SNS websites.

17. On SNS, in which website you feel comfortable?
Table 5.53: Frequency of Millennial according to comfort ability of SNS websites

		Freq.	Per. (%)	Valid %	Cu.%
V	FB	374	72.7	72.7	71.6
	TWT	59	11.5	11.5	84.2
	LIKDN	81	15.8	15.8	100.0
	Total	514	100.0	100.0	

It can be observed from survey result that, from 514 participants , 374 Millennial Information technology professional are feel comfortable on face book, 59 professionals said that they are more comfortable on twitter, 81 Information technology professional said that they see more comfort on LinkedIn when they visiting SNS websites.

On the basis of percentage of 100% participants , 72.7% Millennial Information technology professional are feel comfortable on face book, 11.5% professionals said that they are more comfortable on twitter, 15.8% Information technology professional said that they see more comfort on LinkedIn when they visiting SNS websites.

18. On the basis of method of advertisement for specific group , provide a suitable rating from lowest side to highest side for SNS websites-Face book

Table 5.54: Facebook rating on the basis of method of adv. for specific group

		Freq.	Per. (%)	Valid %	Cu.%
V	1.0	27	5.2	5.2	5.2
	2.0	11	2.3	2.3	7.5
	3.0	18	3.5	3.5	11
	4.0	25	5.1	5.1	16.1
	5.0	37	7.0	7.0	23.1
	6.0	27	5.5	5.5	28.6
	7.0	68	13.2	13.2	41.8
	8.0	91	17.2	17.2	59
	9.0	65	12.5	12.5	71.5
	10.0	149	28.5	28.5	100.0
	Total Participants	514	100.0	100.0	

It can be observed from survey result that, from 514 participants, minimum 11 and maximum 149 Millennial Information technologies professional are find that Facebook is the most suitable site for targeting advertisement on the basis specific group.

On the basis of percentage of 100% participants, minimum 2.3% and maximum 28.5% Millennial Information technology professional are finding that Facebook is the most suitable site for targeting advertisement on the basis specific group.

19. On the basis of method of advertisement for specific group, provide a suitable rating from lowest side to highest side for SNS websites-Twitter

Table 5.55: Twitter rating on the basis of method of adve. for specific group

130

		Freq.	Per. (%)	Valid %	Cu.%
Valid	1.0	23	4.4	4.4	4.4
	2.0	37	7.9	7.9	12.3
	3.0	33	6.8	6.8	19.1
	4.0	63	12.2	12.2	31.3
	5.0	79	15.0	15.0	46.3
	6.0	86	17.4	17.4	63.7
	7.0	57	10.2	10.2	73.9
	8.0	54	11.0	11.0	84.9
	9.0	32	6.8	6.8	91.7
	10.0	50	8.3	8.3	100.0
	Total	514	100.0	100.0	

It can be observed from survey result that, from 514 participants, minimum 23 and maximum 86 Millennial Information technologies professional are find that Twitter is the most suitable site for targeting advertisement on the basis specific group.

On the basis of percentage of 100% participants, minimum 4.4% and maximum 17.4% Millennial Information technology professional are finding that Twitter is the most suitable site for targeting advertisement on the basis specific group.

20. On the basis of method of advertisement for specific group, provide a suitable rating from lowest side to highest side for SNS websites-LinkedIn

Table 5.56: LinkedIn rating on the basis of method of adv. for specific group

		Freq.	Per. (%)	Valid %	Cu.%
V	1	52	10.2	10.2	10.7
	2	91	17.7	17.7	27.9
	3	35	6.8	6.8	34.7
	4	30	6.2	6.2	40.9
	5	41	7.8	7.8	48.7

6	52	10.8	10.8	59.5
7	57	10.6	10.6	70.1
8	48	9.7	9.7	79.8
9	46	9.4	9.4	89.2
10	62	10.8	10.8	100.0
Total	514	100.0	100.0	

It can be observed from survey result that, from 514 participants, minimum 30 and maximum 91 Millennial Information technologies professional are finding that LinkedIn is the most suitable site for targeting advertisement on the basis specific group.

On the basis of percentage of 100% participants, minimum 6.2% and maximum 17.7% Millennial Information technology professional are finding that LinkedIn is the most suitable site for targeting advertisement on the basis specific group.

21. Advertisements on Facebook gives good feeling about products?

Table 5.57: Millennial who have good feeling about products on Facebook?

		Freq.	Per. (%)	Valid %	Cu.%
Valid	Y	410	80.0	80.0	80.0
	N	93	19.9	19.9	99.9
	12.00	1	.1	.1	100.0
	Total participants	514	100.0	100.0	

It can be observed from survey result that, from 514 participants , 410 Millennial Information technology professional are find Advertisements on Facebook gives good feeling about products, 93 professionals not felt that advertisements on Facebook gives good feeling about products.

132

On the basis of percentage of 100% participants, 80% Millennial Information technology professional are find Advertisements on Facebook gives good feeling about products, 19.9% professionals not felt that advertisements on Facebook gives good feeling about products.

22. Advertisements on Twitter gives good feeling about products?

Table 5.58: Millennial who have good feeling about products on Twitter

		Freq.	Per. (%)	Valid %	Cu.%
V	Y	98	19.0	19.0	19.0
	N	415	80.9	99.9	99.0
	10	1	.1	0.1	100
	Total	514	100.0	100.0	

It can be observed from survey result table no. 6.58 that, from 514 participants , 98 Millennial Information technology professional are find Advertisements on Twitter gives good feeling about products, 415 professionals not felt that advertisements on Twitter gives good feeling about products.

On the basis of percentage of 100% participants, 19% Millennial Information technology professional are find Advertisements on Twitter gives good feeling about products, 80.9% professionals not felt that advertisements on Twitter gives good feeling about products.

23. Advertisements on LinkedIn gives good feeling about products?

Table 5.59: Millennial who have good feeling about products on LinkedIn?

		Freq.	Per. (%)	Valid %	Cu.%
V	Y	89	17.3	17.3	17.3
	N	425	82.7	82.7	100.0
	Total Participants	514	100.0	100.0	

It can be observed from survey result that, from 514 participants , 89 Millennial Information technology professional are find Advertisements on LinkedIn gives good feeling about products, 82.7% professionals not felt that advertisements on LinkedIn gives good feeling about products.

On the basis of percentage of 100% participants, 17.3% Millennial Information technology professional are find Advertisements on LinkedIn gives good feeling about products, 429 professionals not felt that advertisements on LinkedIn gives good feeling about products.

24. Advertisements on Facebook motivate you for purchasing?
Table 5.60: Millennial who advertisements on Facebook motivating for purchasing

		Freq.	Per. (%)	Valid %	Cu.%
V	Y	345	67.1	67.1	67.1
	N	169	32.9	32.9	100.0
	Total	514	100.0	100.0	

It can be observed from survey result that, from 514 participants, 345 Millennial Information technology professional are find advertisements on Facebook motivate for purchasing, 169 professionals not feel that advertisements on Facebook motivate for purchasing.

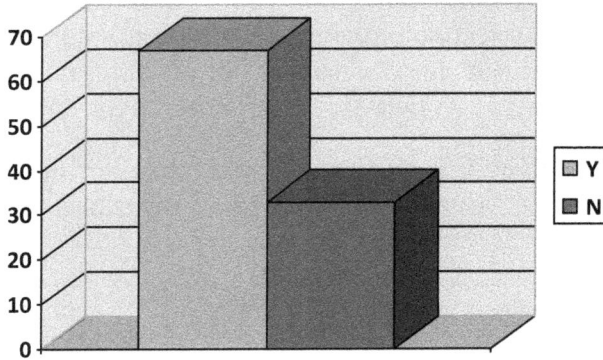

Figure 5.24: Millennial motivated for purchasing
motivated by Facebook

On the basis of percentage of 100% participants, 67.1% Millennial Information technology professional are find advertisements on Facebook motivate for purchasing, 32.9% professionals not feel that advertisements on Facebook motivate for purchasing.

25. Advertisements on twitter motivate you for purchasing?
Table 5.61: Millennial who Advertisements on twitter motivating for purchasing

		Freq.	Per. (%)	Valid %	Cu.%
V	Y	102	19.8	19.8	19.8
	N	412	80.2	80.2	100.0
	Total Participants	514	100.0	100.0	

It can be observed from survey result that, from 514 participants, 102 Millennial Information technology professional are find advertisements on twitter motivate for purchasing, 412 professionals not feel that advertisements on twitter motivate for purchasing.

On the basis of percentage of 100% participants, 19.8% Millennial Information technology professional are find advertisements on twitter motivate for purchasing, 80.2% professionals not feel that advertisements on twitter motivate for purchasing.

26. Advertisements on LinkedIn motivate you for purchasing?
Table 5.62: Millennial who advertisements on LinkedIn motivating for purchasing

		Freq.	Per. (%)	Valid %	Cu.%
V	Y	82	15.9	15.9	15.9
	N	432	84.1	84.1	100.0
	Total Participants	514	100.0	100.0	

It can be observed from survey result that, from 514 participants, 82 Millennial Information technology professional are find advertisements on LinkedIn motivate for purchasing, 432 professionals not feel that advertisements on LinkedIn motivate for purchasing.

On the basis of percentage of 100% participants, 15.9% Millennial Information technology professional are find advertisements on LinkedIn motivate for purchasing, 84.1% professionals not feel that advertisements on LinkedIn motivate for purchasing.

27. Do you find advertisement on Facebook is attractive and memorable?
Table 5.63: Millennial who advertisement on Facebook are attractive and memorable

		Freq.	Per. (%)	Valid %	Cu.%
	Y	354	68.8	68.8	68.8
	N	159	31.1	31.1	99.9
	11.00	1	.1	.1	100.0
	Total Participants	514	100.0	100.0	

It can be observed from survey result that, from 514 participants , 354 Millennial Information technology professional are find advertisement on Facebook are attractive and memorable, 159 professionals not find advertisement on Facebook are attractive and memorable.

On the basis of percentage of 100% participants, 68.8% Millennial Information technology professional are advertisement on Facebook are attractive and memorable, 31.1 % professionals not find advertisement on Facebook are attractive and memorable

28. Do you find advertisements on Twitter are attractive and memorable?

Table 5.64: Millennial who advertisement on twitter are attractive and memorable

		Freq.	Per. (%)	Valid %	Cu.%
V	Y	95	18.4	18.4	18.4
	N	419	81.6	81.6	100.0
	Total Participants	514	100.0	100.0	

It can be observed from survey result that, from 514 participants , 95 Millennial Information technology professional are find advertisement on Twitter are attractive and memorable, 419 professionals not find advertisement on Twitter are attractive and memorable.

On the basis of percentage of 100% participants, 18.4% Millennial Information technology professional are advertisement on Twitter are attractive and memorable, 81.6 % professionals not find advertisement on Twitter are attractive and memorable.

29. Do you find advertisement on LinkedIn is attractive and memorable?

Table 5.65: Millennial who advt. on LinkedIn are attractive and memorable

		Freq.	Per. (%)	Valid %	Cu.%
V	Y	85	16.5	16.5	16.5
	N	429	83.5	83.5	100.0
	Total Participants	514	100.0	100.0	

It can be observed from survey result that, from 514 participants , 85 Millennial Information technology professional are find advertisement on LinkedIn are attractive and memorable, 429 professionals not find advertisement on LinkedIn are attractive and memorable.

On the basis of percentage of 100% participants, 16.5% Millennial Information technology professional are advertisement on LinkedIn are attractive and memorable, 83.5% professionals not find advertisement on LinkedIn are attractive and memorable.

30. Do you find eye-catching advertisement on Facebook?
Table 5.66: Frequency who finds eye-catching advertisement on Facebook.

		Freq.	Per. (%)	Valid %	Cu.%
V	Y	323	62.8	65.8	65.8
	N	191	37.2	34.2	100.0
	Total Participants	514	100.0	100.0	

It can be observed from survey result that, from 514 participants , 323 Millennial Information technology professional are find eye-catching advertisement on Facebook, 191 professionals not find very attractive eye-catching advertisement on Facebook.

On the basis of percentage of 100% participants, 62.8% Millennial Information technology professional are find eye-catching advertisement on Facebook, 34.2% professionals not find very attractive eye-catching advertisement on Facebook.

31. Do you find eye-catching advertisement on Twitter?

Table 5.67: Frequency who finds eye-catching advertisement on Twitter

		Freq.	Per. (%)	Valid %	Cu.%
V	Y	112	21.7	21.7	21.7
	N	402	78.3	78.3	100.0
	Total Participants	514	100.0	100.0	

It can be observed from survey result that, from 514 participants , 112 Millennial Information technology professional are find eye-catching advertisement on Twitter, 402 professionals not find very attractive eye-catching advertisement on Twitter.

On the basis of percentage of 100% participants, 21.7% Millennial Information technology professional are find eye-catching advertisement on Twitter, 78.3% professionals not find very attractive eye-catching advertisement on Twitter.

32. Do you find eye-catching advertisement on LinkedIn?

Table 5.68: Frequency who finds eye-catching advertisement on LinkedIn

		Freq.	Per. (%)	Valid %	Cu.%
V	Y	65	12.6	12.6	12.6
	N	449	87.4	87.4	100.0
	Total Participants	514	100.0	100.0	

It can be observed from survey result that, from 514 participants , 316 Millennial Information technology professional are find eye-catching advertisement on LinkedIn, 198 professionals not find very attractive eye-catching advertisement on LinkedIn.

On the basis of percentage of 100% participants, 12.6% Millennial Information technology professional are find eye-catching advertisement on LinkedIn, 87.4% professionals not find very attractive eye-catching advertisement on LinkedIn.

33. Do you believe on Facebook website advertisement?
Table 5.69: Frequency who believe on Facebook website advertisement

		Freq.	Per. (%)	Valid %	Cu.%
V	Y	316	61.4	61.4	61.4
	N	198	38.6	38.6	100.0
	Total	514	100.0	100.0	

It can be observed from survey result that, from 514 participants , 316 Millennial Information technology professional are believe on Facebook website advertisement, 198 professionals not believed in the advertisements displayed on the Facebook websites.

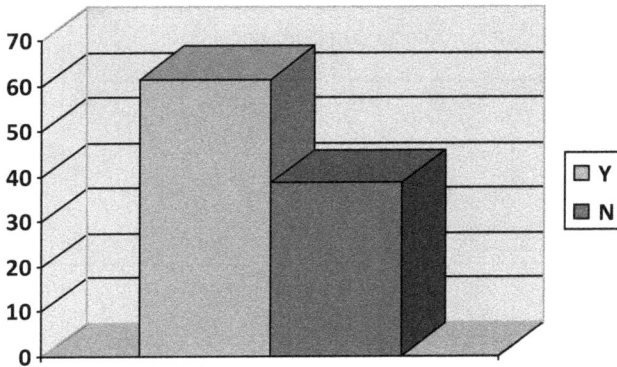

Figure 6.25: Millennial Believe on Facebook Advertisements
On the basis of percentage of 100% participants, 61.4% Millennial Information technology professional are believe on Facebook website advertisement, whereas 38.6 professionals did not believed in the advertisements displayed on the Facebook websites.

34. Do you believe on Twitter website advertisement?
Table 5.70: Frequency of Millennial who believe on Twitter website advertisement

		Freq.	Per. (%)	Valid %	Cu.%
V	Y	89	17.3	17.3	17.3
	N	425	82.6	82.6	99.9
	11	1	.1	.1	100
	Total	514	100.0	100.0	

It can be observed from survey result that, from 514 participants , 85 Millennial Information technology professional are believe on Twitter website advertisement, 429 professionals not believed in the advertisements displayed on the Twitter websites.

On the basis of percentage of 100% participants, 16.4% Millennial Information technology professional are believe on Twitter website advertisement, whereas 83.6 professionals did not believed in the advertisements displayed on the Twitter websites.

35. Do you believe on LinkedIn website advertisement?

Table 5.71: Frequency who believe on LinkedIn website advertisement

		Freq.	Per. (%)	Valid %	Cu.%
V	Y	95	18.4	18.4	18.4
	N	419	81.6	81.6	100.0
	Total Participants	514	100.0	100.0	

It can be observed from survey result that, from 514 participants , 95 Millennial Information technology professional are believe on LinkedIn website advertisement, 419 professionals not believed in the advertisements displayed on the LinkedIn websites.

On the basis of percentage of 100% participants, 18.4% Millennial Information technology professional are believe on LinkedIn website advertisement, whereas 81.6% professionals did not believed in the advertisements displayed on the LinkedIn websites.

36. How many times watch the Advertisements of electronics products, when visit the social networking platform?

Table 5.72: Millennial have seen Advertisements products, when visit the SNA

		Freq.	Per. (%)	Valid %	Cu.%
Valid	Never	46	8.9	8.9	8.9
	1 to 2	159	30.9	30.9	39.8
	3 to 4	184	35.7	35.7	75.5
	4 to 5	90	17.8	17.8	93.3
	Greater then 5	34	6.6	6.6	99.9
	52.00	1	.1	.1	100.0
	Total	514	100.0	100.0	

It can be observed from survey result that, from 514 participants , 46 Millennial Information technology professional are never seen the advertisement of SNS platform, when they visit the internet, 159 professionals believed they watch the advertisement one to two times when visit the sites, 184 Information technology professional said that they visit three to four times at the time of visit the SNS websites,90 IT professional said that they watch the advertisement at the time they visit the social networking website , whereas 34 watch the advertisement more than five times at the time of visiting SNS websites.

On the basis of percentage of 100% participants , 8.9% Millennial Information technology professional are never seen the advertisement of SNS platform, when they visit the internet, 30.9% professionals believed they watch the advertisement one to two times when visit the sites, 35.7% Information technology professional said that they visit three to four times at the time of visit the SNS websites,17.8% IT professional said that they watch the advertisement at the time of visit the social networking website , whereas 6.6% watch the advertisement more than five times at the time of visiting SNS websites.

37. What is the satisfaction level after purchasing of product, inspired by social networking platform Advertisements?

Table5.73: Satisfaction level after purchasing of product, inspired by SNA

		Freq.	Per. (%)	Valid %	Cu.%
V	Very high	82	17.0	17.0	17.0
	high	320	61.3	61.3	78.2
	No	78	16.3	16.3	94.5
	low	26	5.3	5.3	98.8
	Very Low	8	1.2	1.2	100
	Total	514	100	100	

It can be observed from survey result that, from 514 participants , 82 Millennial Information technology professional are feel very high level of satisfaction after purchasing of product, inspired by social networking platform Advertisements, 320 professionals believed that they are satisfied with the purchased products, 78 Information technology professional said that they are not satisfied with the purchased product,26 IT professional said that they are not satisfied with the purchased product after influencing the social media advertisements, whereas 8 very much dissatisfied with the performance of purchased products. On the basis of percentage of 100% participants , 17.0% Millennial Information technology professional are feel very high level of satisfaction after purchasing of production the basis of advertisement on the SNS, 61.3% Information technology professional believed that they are satisfied with the purchased products, 16.3% Information technology professional said that they are not satisfied with the purchased product, 5.3% IT professional said that they are not satisfied with the purchased product after influencing the social media advertisements and 1.2% very much dissatisfied with the performance of purchased products

Objective 5:-To study cultural and geographical forces on Social media advertisement

1. Impact of age on buying behavior of millennial

H01　　There is no significant impact of age on buying behavior of millennial.

H11　　There is no significant impact of age on buying behavior of millennial.

Chi-Sq Test

Table 5.74:　Chi-Sq. test for impact of age on buying behavior of millennial

	Value	df	Asymp. Sig. (2-sided)
Pearson Chi-Square	38.539(a)	6.0	0.0
Likelihood Ratio	33.713	6.0	0.0
Linear-by-Linear	23.274	1.0	0.0
N of Valid Cases	514		

144

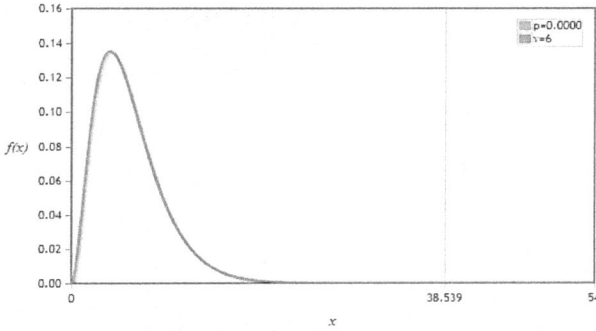

Figure 5.26: Frequently used Website for purchasing

If X is a random variable having a $\chi2$ distribution with $v = 6$ degrees of freedom, then $p = \Pr[X \geq 38.539] = 0.0000$.

By the Chi-Sq. test analysis, find out that the 5% significance Level ($P < \alpha$) and on the basis Null hypo. May be not valid and subsequently other alternative may be accepted. So on the basis of study there is relation between the two factors i.e. "impact of age" with buying behavior of IT Professional for electronics products. This means the factor i.e. "impact of age" buying behavior of millennial IT Professional in Indore for electronics products having dependency with both factors.

Table of Symmetric Measures(SM)

Table 5.75: SM for measuring the relation between impacts of age

		Amount	Approx. Significance
Nom. By Nom	Coeff. Of Cont.	0.767	0.00
Valid Numbers		514	

By the analysis of above SM table, strong positive relation between the buying behavior of IT Professional for electronics products and impact of age and around 76.7 percent it can be affect.

2. Impact of annual income on buying behavior of millennial

H02 There is no significant impact of income on buying behavior of millennial.

H12 There is significant impact of income on buying behavior of millennial

Chi-Square Tests

Table 6.76: Chi-Sq. test for the impact of income

	Value	df	Asymp. Sig. (2-sided)
Pearson Chi-Square	32.546(a)	28	.374
Likelihood Ratio	32.343	28	.375
Linear-by-Linear	5.365	1	.023
Number of valid participants	514		

If X is a random variable having a $\chi2$ distribution with $v = 28$ degrees of freedom, then $p = \Pr[X \geq 32.546] = 0.2529$.

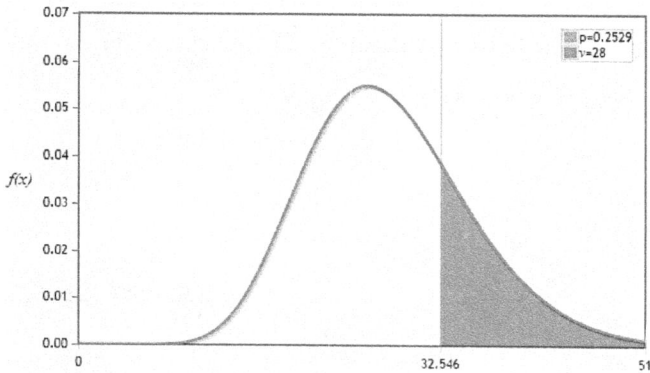

Figure 5.27: Distribution chart for impact of income

By the Chi-Sq. test analysis, find out that the 5% significance Level (P < α) and on the basis Null hypo. May be not valid and subsequently other alternative may be accepted. So on the basis of study there is relation between the two factor i.e. "impact of income" with buying behavior of IT Professional for electronics products . This means the factor i.e. "impact of income" buying behaviour of millennial IT Professional in Indore for electronics products having dependency with both factors. CCS (Contingency Coefficient Statistics) will use for measuring the amount of further relationship.

Symmetric Measures

Table 5.77: Symmetric measures for relationship exists between impact of income

		Value	App. Sign
N by N	P and C value	.667	0.00
Valid Cases		514	

Results from the above table showed that the significant impact of income and buying behavior of millennial and it will affect around 66.7 %

3. Impact of gender on buying behavior of millennial

H03   There is no significant impact of gender on buying behavior of millennial.

H13   There is significant impact of gender on buying behavior of millennial

Chi-Square Tests

Table 5.78: Chi-Sq. test for the Impact of gender

	Value	df	Asymp. Sig. (2-sided)
Pearson Chi-Square	25.151-a	6	0.0890
Likelihood Ratio	25.876	6	0.0545
Linear-by-Linear	21.771	1	0.332
Number of valid participants	514		

If X is a random variable having a $\chi 2$ distribution with $v = 6$ degrees of freedom, then $p = \Pr[X \geq 25.151] = 0.0003$.

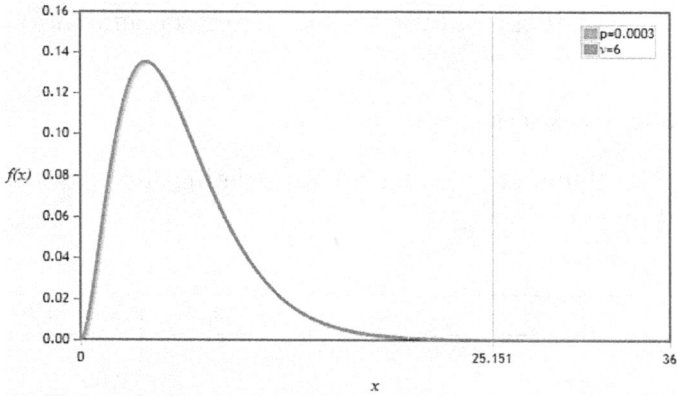

Figure 5.28: Distribution chart for impact of gender

By the Chi-Sq. test analysis, find out that the 5% significance Level (P < α) and on the basis Null hypo. Valid and subsequently other alternative may be not accepted. So on the basis of study there is relation between the two factors i.e. "impact of gender" with buying behaviour of IT Professional for electronics products. . This means the factor i.e. "impact of gender" with buying behaviour of IT Professional for electronics products.having no dependency with both factors.

ANOVA

Table 5.79: ANOVA Relationship of gender of millennial

	Sum of Squares	Df	Mean Square	F	Sig.
Between Groups	.161	2	.080	2.065	.128
Within Groups	19.968	513	.039		
Total	20.129	515			

From the above table, it is observed that p > α (0.05), so the null hypothesis is accepted and alternative is rejected, so we can conclude that impact of social media advertising and the Occupation of millennial are independent of each other. So, we can say that social media advertisement does not have any impact on gender of the millennial.

4. Impact of education on buying behavior of millennial

H04   There is no significant impact of education on buying behavior of millennial.

H14   There is significant impact of education on buying behavior of millennial

Chi-Square Tests

Table 5.80: Chi-Sq. test for the impact of education

	Value	df	Asymp. Sig. (2-sided)
Pearson Chi-Square	25.652(a)	15	.374
Likelihood Ratio	25.462	15	.375
Linear-by-Linear Association	6.421	1	.023
Number of valid participants	514		

If X is a random variable having a $\chi 2$ distribution with $v = 15$ degrees of freedom, then $p = \Pr[X \geq 25.652] = 0.0418$.

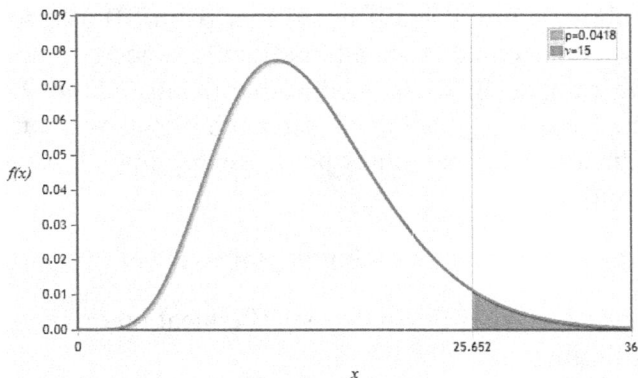

Figure 5.29: Distribution chart for impact of education

By the Chi-Sq. test analysis, find out that the 5% significance Level(P < α) and on the basis Null hypo. May be not valid and subsequently other alternative may be accepted. So on the basis of study there is relation between the two factor i.e. "impact of education" with buying behavior of IT Professional for electronics products . This means the factor i.e. "impact of education" buying behaviour of millennial IT Professional in Indore for electronics products having dependency with both factors. CCS (Contingency Coefficient Statistics) will use for measuring the amount of further relationship.

Symmetric Measures

Table 6.81: Symmetric measures for relationship exists between impact of education

		Value	App. Sign
N by N	P and C value	.542	0.00
Valid Cases		514	

Results from the above table showed that relationship exists between impact of education and buying behavior of millennial and it will affect around 54.2 %.

5. Impact of cultural and geographical forces on buying behavior of millennial

H05   There is no significant impact of cultural and geographical forces on buying behavior of millennial.
H15   There is significant impact of cultural and geographical forces on buying behavior of millennial

Chi-Square Tests

Table 5.82: Chi-Sq. test for the impact of cultural and geographical forces

	Value	df	Asymp. Sig. (2-sided)
Pearson Chi-Square	28.964-a	15	.876
Likelihood Ratio	29.659	15	.854
Linear-by-Linear	2.853	1	.086
Number of valid participants	514		

If X is a random variable having a $\chi 2$ distribution with $v = 15$ degrees of freedom, then $p = \Pr[X \geq 28.964] = 0.0163$.

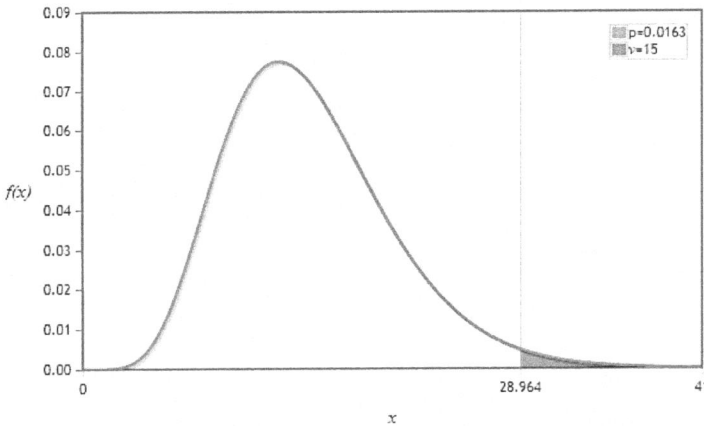

Figure 5.30: Distribution chart for impact of geographical forces

By the Chi-Sq. test analysis, find out that the 5% significance Level(P < α) and on the basis Null hypo. valid and subsequently other alternative may be not accepted. So on the basis of study there is relation between the two factor i.e. cultural and geographical forces" with buying behaviour of IT Professional for electronics products. This means the factor i.e. "cultural and geographical forces" buying behaviour of millennial IT Professional in Indore for electronics products having no dependency with both factors.

Objective 6: To study impact of social media advertisement on perception of Millennial while they purchase electronic gadgets.

1. Relationship between complex buying behaviour with the factor of Social Media Advertisement i.e. "On which social networking sites millennial trust the advertisement displayed" –

H0: There is no association between the factors i.e. "On which social networking sites millennial trust the advertisement displayed" with Complex buying behaviour of millennial for consumer electronics.

H1: There is association between the factors i.e. "On which social networking sites millennial trust the advertisement displayed" with Complex buying behaviour of millennial for consumer electronics

Chi-Square Tests

Table 5.83: Relationship between complex buying behaviour with the trust factor of social media advertising.

	Value	Df	Asymp.Sig.(2-sided)
Pearson Chi-Square	42.121(a)	8	.000
Likelihood Ratio	56.77	8	.000
Linear-by-Linear	18.778	1	.000
N of Valid Cases	514		

If X is a random variable having a $\chi2$ distribution with $v = 8$ degrees of freedom, then $p = \Pr[X \geq 42.121] = 0.0000$.

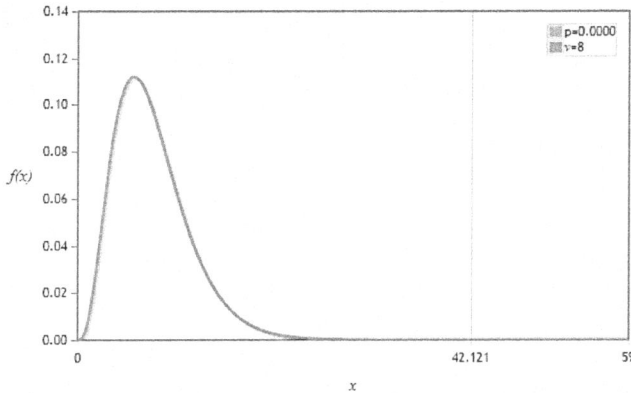

Figure 5.31: Distribution chart for complex behaviour

From the above table, it is observed at 5 % level of significance p <
α (0.05), so the null hypothesis rejected and alternative is accepted,
so, we conclude that there is association between the factor i.e. "On
which social networking sites millennial trust the advertisement
displayed" with Complex buying behaviour of millennial for
consumer electronics . This means the factor i.e. "On which social
networking sites millennial trust the advertisement displayed" with
Complex buying behaviour of millennial for consumer electronics
because they are dependent of each other for. Further to check how
much association is exist we will use the Contingency Coefficient
Statistics.

Symmetric Measures

Table 6.84: A symmetric measure for relationship between
complex behaviour and the trust

		Value	Approx. Sig.
Nominal by Nominal	Contingency Coefficient	.860	.000
N of Valid Cases		514	

From the above table, it is observed that they are having very strong trust towards advertisements displayed on social media for buying electronics products, which will affect complex buying behaviour 86.0 %.

2. Relationship between all the factors of Variety Seeking Buying Behaviour with all the factor of Social Media Advertisement –

H0 : All the factors of Social Media Advertisement and all the factors of Variety Seeking Buying Behaviour of millennial for consumer electronics are independent of each other.

H1 : All the factors of Social Media Advertisement and all the factors of Variety Seeking Buying Behaviour of millennial for consumer electronics are dependent of each other.

ANOVA

Table 5.85: Relationship between all the factors of variety seeking behaviour and all the factors of social media advertising.

	Sum of Square	Df	Mean square	F	Sig.
Between Groups	3.626	9	.403	6.832	.000
Within Groups	29.838	506	.059		
Total	33.464	515			

From the above table, it is observed that $p < \alpha$ (0.05), so the null hypothesis is rejected and alternative is accepted, so we can conclude that all the factors of Social Media Advertisement and all the factors of Variety Seeking Buying Behaviour of millennial for consumer electronics are dependent of each other. So, we can say that social media advertisement have an impact on Variety Seeking Buying Behaviour of the millennial.

3. Relationship between all the factors of Dissonance Buying Behaviour with all the factor of Social Media Advertisement –

H0: All the factors of Social Media Advertisement and all the factors of Dissonance Buying Behaviour of millennial for consumer electronics are independent of each other.

H1: All the factors of Social Media Advertisement and all the factors of Dissonance Buying Behaviour of millennial for consumer electronics are dependent of each other.

ANOVA

Table 5.86: ANOVAs relationship between all the factors of Dissonance buying behaviour and all the factors of social media advertising.

	Sum of Squares	Df	Mean Square	F	Sig.
Between Groups	1.914	9	.213	3.411	.000
Within Groups	31.550	506	.062		
Total	33.464	515			

From the above table, it is observed that $p < \alpha$ (0.05), so the null hypothesis is rejected and alternative is accepted, so we can conclude that all the factors of Social Media Advertisement and all the factors of Dissonance Buying Behaviour of millennial for consumer electronics are dependent of each other. So, we can say that social media advertisement have an impact on Dissonance Buying Behaviour of the millennial.

155

4. Relationship between all the factors of Impulsive Buying Behaviour with all the factor of Social Media Advertisement –

H0: All the factors of Social Media Advertisement and all the factors of Impulsive Buying Behaviour of millennial for consumer electronics are independent of each other.

H1: All the factors of Social Media Advertisement and all the factors of Impulsive Buying Behaviour of millennial for consumer electronics are dependent of each other.

ANOVA

Table 5.87: ANOVAs relationship between all the factors of Impulsive buying behaviour and all the factors of social media advertising.

	Sum of Squares	Df	Mean Square	F	Sig.
Between Groups	.979	10	.098	1.522	.128
Within Groups	32.484	505	.064		
Total	33.464	515			

From the above table, it is observed that $p > \alpha$ (0.05), so the null hypothesis is accepted and alternative is rejected, so we can conclude that all the factors of Social Media Advertisement and all the factors of Impulsive Buying Behaviour of millennial for consumer electronics are independent of each other. So, we can say that social media advertisement does not have an impact on Impulsive Buying Behaviour of the millennial.

5. Relationship between impact of social media advertising of millennial with their Annual Income –

H0: Impact of social media advertising and the Annual Income of millennial are independent of each other

156

H1: Impact of social media advertising and the Annual Income of millennial are dependent of each other

ANOVA

Table 5.88: ANOVAs relationship of annual income of millennial

	Sum of Squares	Df	Mean Square	F	S
Between Groups	.040	3	.013	.339	.7
Within Groups	20.089	512	.039		
Total	20.129	515			

From the above table, it is observed that p > α (0.05), so the null hypothesis is accepted and alternative is rejected, so we can conclude that impact of social media advertising and the Annual Income of millennial are independent of each other. So, we can say that social media advertisement does not have any impact on Annual Income of the millennial.

6. Relationship between At the time of accessing internet how much time you spend on SNS - Any Other

Table 5.90: At the time of accessing internet how much time spends on SNS.

		Freq.	Per. (%)	Valid %	Cu.%
V	15 min	68	13.2	13.2	13.2
	30 min	143	27.8	28.1	41.0
	1 hr.	192	37.3	35.1	78.3
	2 hr	95	18.4	17.5	96.7
	Greater than 2 hr. HOURS	16	3.3	3.3	100.0
	Total Participants	514	100.0	100.0	

It can be observed from survey result that, from 514 participants, 68 Millennial Information technology professional are spending time on another sites,15 minute at the time of accessing internet, 143 Millennial Information technology professional are spending 30 minute at the time of accessing internet, 192 professionals agreed that they are spending 1hour at the time of accessing internet, 95 Information technology professional said that spending 1hour at the time of accessing internet and 16 IT professionals spending time more than 2hour.

On the basis of percentage of 100% participants, 13.2% Millennial Information technology professional are spending 15 minute at the time of accessing internet, 28.1%Millennial Information technology professional are spending 30 minute at the time of accessing internet, 37.3% professionals agreed that they are spending 1hour at the time of accessing internet, 18.4% Information technology professional said that spending 1hour at the time of accessing internet and 3.3% IT professionals spending time more than 2 hour.

7. Spending Time on SNS compared to previous year-IS it Less, More, No change

Table 5.91: Spending time on SNS compared to previous year

		Freq.	Per. (%)	Valid %	Cu.%
V	More	204	39.6	39.6	39.6
	Less	176	34.2	34.2	73.8
	No change same	134	26.2	26.2	100.0
	Total	514	100.0	100.0	

It can be observed from survey result that, from 514 participants, 204 Millennial Information technology professional are spending more time on SNS compared to previous year, 176 Millennial Information technology professional are spending less Time on SNS compared to previous year, 134 professionals agreed that no change in spending Time on SNS compared to previous year.

On the basis of percentage of 100% participants, 39..6% Millennial Information technology professional are spending more time on SNS compared to previous year, 34.2% Millennial Information technology professional are spending less time on SNS compared to previous year , 26.2% professionals agreed that no change in spending time on SNS compared to previous year.

8. Spending time for Product information on SNS compared to previous year-IS it More ,Less, No change

Table 5.92: Spending time for Product information on SNS compared to previous year

		Freq.	Per. (%)	Valid %	Cu.%
V	More	116	22.6	22.6	22.6
	Less	325	63.2	63.2	85.8
	No change	73	14.2	14.2	100.0
	Total	514	100.0	100.0	

It can be observed from survey result that, from 514 participants, 116Millennial Information technology professional are spending more time for Product information on SNS compared to previous year, 325 Millennial Information technology professional are spending less Time for Product information on SNS compared to previous year, 73 professionals agreed that no change in spending Time for Purchasing the product on SNS compared to previous year.

On the basis of percentage of 100% participants, 22..6% Millennial Information technology professional are spending more Time for Product information on SNS compared to previous year, 63.2% Millennial Information technology professional are spending less Time for Product information on SNS compared to previous year , 14.2% professionals agreed that no change in spending Time for Purchasing the product on SNS compared to previous year

9. Spending Time for Purchasing the product on SNS compared to previous year-IS it more, less, No change?

Table 5.93: Spending time for the product on SNS compared to previous year

		Freq.	Per. (%)	Valid %	Cu.%
V	More	229	44.7	44.7	44.7
	Less	168	32.6	32.6	77.3
	No change time	117	22.7	22.7	100.0
	Total Participants	514	100.0	100.0	

It can be observed from survey result that, from 514 participants, 229 Millennial Information technology professional are spending more Time for Purchasing the product on SNS compared to previous year , 168 Millennial Information technology professional are spending less Time for Purchasing the product on SNS compared to previous year , 117 professionals agreed that no change in spending Time for Purchasing the product on SNS compared to previous year.

On the basis of percentage of 100% participants, 44.7% Millennial Information technology professional are spending more Time for Purchasing the product on SNS compared to previous year, 32.6% Millennial Information technology professional are spending less Time for Purchasing the product on SNS compared to previous year, 22.7% professionals agreed that no change in spending Time for Purchasing the product on SNS compared to previous year.

10. Are you interested to sharing the product feedback with family and friends?

Table 5.94: Millennial that interested to sharing feedback with family and friends

		Freq.	Per. (%)	Valid %	Cu.%
V	Y	254	49.4	49.4	49.4
	N	260	50.6	50.6	100.0

	Total Participants	514	100.0	100.0	

It can be observed from survey result that, from 514 participants, 254 Millennial Information technology professional are interested to sharing the product feedback with family and friends, 260 professionals not interested to sharing the product feedback with family and friends

On the basis of percentage of 100% participants, only 49.4% Millennial Information technology professional are interested to sharing the product feedback with family and friends, 50.6 % professionals are not interested to sharing the product feedback with family and friends.

11. Are you interested to sharing the product feedback with company?

Table 5.95: Millennial that interested to sharing the feedback with company

		Freq.	Per. (%)	Valid %	Cu.%
V	Y	267	51.9	51.9	51.9
	N	247	48.1	48.1	100.0
	Total	514	100.0	100.0	

It can be observed from survey result that, from 514 participants, 267 Millennial Information technology professional are interested to sharing the product feedback with company, 247 professionals not interested to sharing the product feedback with company.

On the basis of percentage of 100% participants, only 51.9% Millennial Information technology professional are interested to sharing the product feedback with company, 48.1 % professionals are not interested to sharing the product feedback with company

12. Are you visited any shop for providing online rating?.

Table 5.96: Frequency of Millennial who visited any shop for providing online rating

		Freq.	Per. (%)	Valid %	Cu.%
V	Y	276	53.6	53.6	53.6
	N	237	46.3	46.3	99.9
	12.00	1	.1	.1	100.0
	Total	514	100.0	100.0	

It can be observed from survey result that, from 514 participants,276 Millennial Information technology professional are visited any shop for providing online rating , 237 professionals not visited any shop for providing online rating.

On the basis of percentage of 100% participants, only 53.6% Millennial Information technology professional are visited any shop for providing online rating , 46.3 % professionals are not visited any shop for providing online rating.

13. In one year how many times you provide online rating?

Table 5.97: Frequency of Millennial who provides online rating in one year

		Freq.	Per. (%)	Valid %	Cu.%
V	Never rate	276	53.6	53.6	53.6
	Up to 10 times times	185	35.9	35.9	89.5
	11-20 times	29	5.7	5.7	95.2
	21-50 times	15	2.9	2.9	98.1
	More than 50 times	9	1.9	1.9	100.0
	Total	514	100.0	100.0	

It can be observed from survey result that, from 514 participants, 276 Millennial Information technology professional are provides never online rating, 185 Millennial Information technology professional are provides online rating up to 10 times in one year , 29 professionals agreed that provides 11 to 20 times online rating in one year , 15 Information technology professional said that provides21 to 50 times online rating in one year and 9 IT professionals gives online rating more than 50 times.

On the basis of percentage of 100% participants, 53.6% Millennial Information technology professional are provides online rating in one year, 35.9.% Millennial Information technology professional are provides online rating up to 10 times in one year , 5.7% professionals agreed that provides 11 to 20 times online rating in one year , 2.9% Information technology professional said that provides21 to 50 times online rating in one year and 1.%9 IT professionals gives online rating more than 50 times.

14. Are you interested forward the website link particular product to your friends or family?

Table 5.98: Millennial who forward the product website link to your friends or family

		Freq.	Per. (%)	Valid %	Cu.%
V	Y	283	55.2	55.2	55.2
	N	231	44.8	44.8	100.0
	Total Participants	514	100.0	100.0	

It can be observed from survey result that, from 514 participants, 283 Millennial Information technology professional are forward the website link particular product to your friends or family, 231 professionals not forward the website link particular product to your friends or family.

On the basis of percentage of 100% participants, It can be observed from survey result that, from 514 participants, only 55.2% Millennial Information technology professional are forward the website link particular product to your friends or family , 44.8 %

professionals are not forward the website link particular product to your friends or family

15. Have you purchased any consumer electronic items (like Music players, Television set, Video recorder, DVD players, Digital cameras, Personal computers, Telephones, Mobile phones, Video games consoles, camcorders) through social media?

Table 5.99: Millennial purchased electronic items through SNS advertisements

		Freq.	Per. (%)	Valid %	Cu.%
Valid	Y	272	52.9	52.9	52.9
	N	241	47.0	47.0	99.8
	3.00	1	.1	.1	100.0
	Total participants	514	100.0	100.0	

It can be observed from survey result that, from 514 participants, 272 Millennial Information technology professional are purchased electronic items through SNS advertisements , 241 professionals not purchased electronic items through SNS advertisements.

On the basis of percentage of 100% participants, It can be observed from survey result that, from 514 participants, only 52.9% Millennial Information technology professional are purchased electronic items through SNS advertisements , 47 % professionals not are purchased electronic items through SNS advertisements.

16. If yes, reason behind purchasing through SNS platform advertisements?

Table 5.100 list of reason behind purchasing through SNS platform advertisements

		Freq.	Per. (%)	Valid %	Cu.%
Valid	Customer Feedback	142	27.6	27.6	27.6
	Advertisement on SNS	330	64.20	64.20	91.8
	None Any Other	42	8.2	8.2	100.0
	Total	514	100.0	100.0	

It can be observed from survey result that, from 514 participants, 142 Millennial Information technology professional are agreed that the customer feedback is reason behind purchasing through SNS platform advertisements, 330 professionals agreed that the advertisement on social networking sites is reason behind purchasing through SNS platform advertisements, 42 IT professional said no reason behind purchase decision.

On the basis of percentage of 100% participants, 27.6% Millennial Information technology professional are agreed that the customer feedback is reason behind purchasing through SNS platform advertisements, 64.20% professionals agreed that the advertisement on social networking sites is reason behind purchasing through SNS platform advertisements, 8.2% Information technology professional said no reason behind purchase decision .

17. Are you interested to provide online customer rating? - music players.

Table 5.101: Interested to provide online customer rating of music players

		Frequency	Freq.	Per. (%)	Valid %
V	Y	54	10.5	10.5	10.5
	N	460	89.5	89.5	100.0
	Total	514	100.0	100.0	

It can be observed from survey result that, from 514 participants, 54 millennial Information technology professional are interested to provide online customer rating of music players, 460 professionals not interested to provide online customer rating of music players.

On the basis of percentage of 100% participants, It can be observed from survey result that, from 514 participants, only 10.5% Millennial Information technology professional are interested to provide online customer rating of music players, 89.5% professionals not interested to provide online customer rating of music players.

18. Are you interested to provide online customer rating? - TV

Table 5.102: Interested to provide online customer rating of TV

		Freq.	Per. (%)	Valid %	Cu.%
V	Y	69	13.4	13.4	12.7
	N	445	86.6	86.6	100.0
	Total	514	100.0	100.0	

It can be observed from survey result that, from 514 participants,69 Millennial Information technology professional are interested to provide online customer rating of Television, 445 professionals not interested to provide online customer rating of Television.

On the basis of percentage of 100% participants, It can be observed from survey result that, from 514 participants, only 13.4% Millennial Information technology professional are interested to provide online customer rating of Television, 86.6% professionals not interested to provide online customer rating of Television.

19. Are you interested to provide online customer rating?-Video Recorder.

Table 5.103: Interested to provide online customer rating of video recorder

		Freq.	Per. (%)	Valid %	Cu.%
V	Y	45	8.7	8.7	8.7
	N	469	91.3	91.3	100.0
	Total Participants	514	100.0	100.0	

It can be observed from survey result that, from 514 participants,45Millennial Information technology professional are interested to provide online customer rating of video recorder, 469 professionals not interested to provide online customer rating of video recorder.

On the basis of percentage of 100% participants, It can be observed from survey result that, from 514 participants, only 8.7% Millennial Information technology professional are interested to provide online customer rating of video recorder, 91.3% professionals not interested to provide online customer rating of video recorder.

20. Are you interested to provide online customer rating?-- DVD Players.

Table 5.104: Interested to provide online customer rating of DVD player

		Freq.	Per. (%)	Valid %	Cu.%
V	Y	56	10.8	10.8	10.8
	N	458	89.2	89.2	100.0
	Total Participants	514	100.0	100.0	

It can be observed from survey result that, from 514 participants,56 Millennial Information technology professional are interested to provide online customer rating of DVD player , 458 professionals not interested to provide online customer rating of DVD player.

On the basis of percentage of 100% participants, It can be observed from survey result that, from 514 participants, only 10.8% Millennial Information technology professional are interested to provide online customer rating of DVD player , 89.2% professionals not interested to provide online customer rating of DVD player

21. Are you interested to provide online customer rating.- Digital Cameras

Table 5.105: Interested to provide online customer rating of Digital Camera

		Freq.	Per. (%)	Valid %	Cu.%
V	Y	92	17.9	17.9	17.9
	N	422	82.1	82.1	100.0
	Total Participants	514	100.0	100.0	

It can be observed from survey result that, from 514 participants,92 Millennial Information technology professional are interested to provide online customer rating of Digital Camera, 422 professionals not interested to provide online customer rating of Digital Camera.

On the basis of percentage of 100% participants, It can be observed from survey result that, from 514 participants, only 17.9% Millennial Information technology professional are interested to provide online customer rating of Digital Camera, 82.1% professionals not interested to provide online customer rating of Digital Camera.

22. Are you interested to provide online customer rating?.- Personal computers/Laptops.

Table 5.106: Interested to provide online customer rating of computers & laptops

		Freq.	Per. (%)	Valid %	Cu.%
V	Y	138	26.8	26.8	26.8
	N	376	73.2	73.2	100.0
	Total Participants	514	100.0	100.0	

It can be observed from survey result that, from 514 participants, 138 millennial Information technology professional are interested to provide online customer rating of personal computers & laptops, 376 professionals not interested to provide online customer rating of personal computers & laptops.

On the basis of percentage of 100% participants, It can be observed from survey result that, from 514 participants, only 26.8% millennial Information technology professional are interested to provide online customer rating of personal computers & laptops, 73.2% professionals not interested to provide online customer rating of personal computers & laptops.

23. Are you interested to provide online customer rating?- telephone

Table 5.107: Interested to provide online customer rating of telephone instruments

		Freq.	Per. (%)	Valid %	Cu.%
V	Y	65	12.6	12.6	12.6
	N	449	87.4	87.4	100.0
	Total Participants	514	100.0	100.0	

It can be observed from survey result that, from 514 participants,65 Millennial Information technology professional are interested to provide online customer rating of telephone instruments, 449 professionals not interested to provide online customer rating of telephone instruments.

On the basis of percentage of 100% participants, It can be observed from survey result that, from 514 participants, only 12.6% Millennial Information technology professional are interested to

provide online customer rating of telephone instruments, 87.4%
professionals not interested to provide online customer rating   of
telephone instruments.

24. Are you interested to provide online customer rating?-
Mobile Phones.

Table 5.108: Interested to provide online customer rating   of
mobile phones

		Freq.	Per. (%)	Valid %	Cu.%
V	Y	232	45.1	45.1	45.1
	N	282	54.9	54.9	100.0
	Total Participants	514	100.0	100.0	

It can be observed from survey result that, from 514 participants,
232 Millennial Information technology professional are interested
to provide online customer rating of mobile phones, 282
professionals not interested to provide online customer rating   of
mobile phones.

On the basis of percentage of 100% participants, It can be observed
from survey result that, from 514 participants, only 45.1%
Millennial Information technology professional are interested to
provide online customer rating   of mobile phones, 54.9%
professionals not interested to provide online customer rating   of
mobile phones.

25. Are you interested to provide online customer rating? -Video
Games

Table 5.109: Interested to provide online customer rating   of
videogames

		Freq.	Per. (%)	Valid %	Cu.%
V	Y	21	4.1	4.1	4.1
	N	493	95.9	95.9	100.0
	Total Participants	514	100.0	100.0	

It can be observed from survey result that, from 514 participants, 21 Millennial Information technology professional are interested to provide online customer rating of videogames, 493 professionals not interested to provide online customer rating of videogames.

On the basis of percentage of 100% participants, It can be observed from survey result that, from 514 participants, only 4.1% Millennial Information technology professional are interested to provide online customer rating of videogames, 95.9% professionals not interested to provide online customer rating of videogames.

26. Are you interested to provide online customer rating? - Camcorders.

Table 5.110: Interested to provide online customer rating of Camcorders

		Freq.	Per. (%)	Valid %	Cu.%
V	Y	54	10.5	10.5	10.5
	N	460	89.5	89.5	100.0
	Total Participants	514	100.0	100.0	

It can be observed from survey result that, from 514 participants, 366 Millennial Information technology professional are interested to provide online customer rating of Camcorders, 460 professionals not interested to provide online customer rating of Camcorders.

On the basis of percentage of 100% participants, It can be observed from survey result that, from 514 participants, only 10.5% Millennial Information technology professional are interested to provide online customer rating   of Camcorders, 89.5% professionals not interested to provide online customer rating of Camcorders.

27. Are you study customer reviews before purchasing?

Table 5.111: Frequency of Millennial who study customer reviews before purchasing

	Freq.	Per. (%)	Valid %	Cu.%

V	Y	366	71.2	71.2	71.2
	N	148	28.8	28.8	100.0
	Total Ps	514	100.0	100.0	

It can be observed from survey result that, from 514 participants, 366 Millennial Information technology professional are agreed that they study customer reviews before purchasing, 148 professionals not study customer reviews before purchasing. On the basis of percentage of 100% participants, 71.2% Millennial Information technology professional are agreed that they study customer reviews before purchasing, 28.8% professionals not study customer reviews before purchasing.

Chapter 6

Conclusion

The availability of internet and growth of social media implies that, Indore city is growing day by day and the millennial playing an important role for growth of online activity of consumer and taking a help of social media and online source for purchasing of consumer electronics. This is the sign that traditional marketing policies and rules are changing and companies have requirement of new strategy and policies not only in metro city but as well as non-metro city like Indore also.

Following conclusion extracted from detailed research about impact of social media advertisement on millennial.

Association between impacts of social media advertisement on information technology millennial in respect of age

By the analysis of study revealed that there is strong relationship between the impact of social media advertisement on millennial and the age of the professional. The impact of social media advertisement more followed on age between 25 to 30 age group and 18-25 age group and less impact on up to 35 age.

Association between impacts of social media advertisement on information technology millennial in respect of annual income

By the analysis of study revealed that there is strong relationship between the impact of social media advertisement on millennial and the annual income of the professional. The impact of social media advertisement more followed on annual income up to 3 lakh then up to 5 lakhs and minimum impact found on the annual income up to 10 lakhs

Association between impacts of social media advertisement on information technology millennial in respect of gender

By the analysis of study revealed that there is no relationship between the impact of social media advertisement on millennial and the gender of the information technology professional.

Association between impacts of social media advertisement on information technology millennial in respect of annual income

By the analysis of study revealed that there is moderate relationship between the impact of social media advertisement on millennial and the educational qualification of the information technology professional. The impact of social media advertisement more followed on graduate educated then postgraduate and minimum impact found on the certificate level education background.

Various determinants influence the buying behavior of Millennial on social media advertising.

By the analysis of study revealed that several factor influence the buying behavior of the millennial , as per study frequency of use of Social networking sites, type of social networking sites, online review available on the different platform, print and television media, websites of products are the several factor , which influence the final decision of millennial about purchasing any product.

Drivers, motives, reasons and factors affecting the buying behaviors of Millennial.

By the analysis of study revealed that several drivers, motives and reasons affect the buying behavior of the millennial like Personnel Involvement level, available online price, spending time on social media network, frequency of visit advertisement, brand, brand reputation, price comparison with other brand, product attribute, product quality, function ability, value, worth and previous relationship and experience with brand.

Theme and appeal which influence the buying behavior of Millennial

By the analysis of study revealed that social networking sites theme and appeal influence the buying behavior of the millennial. From the research find out that some factor like lucrative advertisement, attractive advertisement, objective of use of social networking sites, easy to use, eye catching ad., satisfaction level after use, attractive and memorable advertisements influence the buying behavior of millennial.

174

Cultural and geographical forces on Social media advertisement

Study showed that cultural and geographical forces influence the buying behavior of the millennial and considerable relationship between the social media advertisement , cultural and geographical forces and buying behavior in case on millennial.

Impact of social media advertisement on perception of Millennial while they purchase electronic gadgets.

By the result of study facts reveled that there are strong effect of social media advertisement on the perception of millennial and some factor like online rating, spending time on social networking time, positive feedback from colleagues and friends, brand value important for perception of millennial buying behavior but it also change according to the type of consumer electronics product, with laptop the perception and behavior will be change whereas with mobile or camera the perception and behavior will quite change.

Chapter 7

Recommendations and Suggestions

7.1   Recommendations and Suggestions:

Now a days the internet spreading all over the world and in India also the online user are increased in the non-metro cities like Indore and even rural areas of country, With the availability of internet and exposure of different products and quality present marketing polices are not very effective. This problem increased when the customer is millennial and online user because online user comparing the products with world class quality and comparing the online customer reviews and satisfaction level of existing customers.

So in the time technological advancement and competition, every business needs specific and competitive marketing strategies for retain market share and increase profit of business. In present time the most promising and technical marketing strategy required, which is based on the social media advertisement with higher efficiency and customer satisfaction level. According to the need the research result is very significant and useful for development of new marketing strategy especially non metro cities like Indore.

Research results showed that the effectiveness of social media advertisement of LinkedIn and twitter is less than popular sites like Facebook, the basic reason behind that this sites should be easy to use, compatibility with customer, trust, emphasis on eye catching advertisement and customer need lots of engaging platform on your websites like gaming, content sharing. Secondly the grouping or demographic feature should be attractive so that customer can spend more time on sites.

Another fact is that millennial earning up to 3lakhs annum are more interested in the social media advertisement, so the products and finance scheme should be for this group more than other group like up to 10 lakh per annum salary and result reveled that there is no connection between the gender on the effect of the social media advertisement effectiveness, so companies can create common advertisement rather than more emphasis on male or female

Basically social media has been internet based innovation for creating and maintaining social network only and common thinking that education is not playing very good role in effectiveness of advertisement but results showed that the below graduate level giving less attention on social media advertisement whereas graduate and post graduate taking seriously social media advertisements.

Now everything depends on the internet and daily life is fully dependent on the availability of internet and social media platform creating an online circle of family and friends, so in the next few decades business, social network will be a big internet hub of all purchasing and related activity. So appearance, theme of website should be good and impressive for customer and its affects the buying behavior of the customer.

7.2   Future Scope of Study:

1. The study can be done in other segment like home appliances, real states, and electrical items
2. Similar study can be done in other non-metro cities or rural areas.
3. Similar study can be done on the different age groups.
4. The study can be done with other group of people.
5. The study area can be change from social networking sites to websites of the product.

APPENDIX

www.ingramcontent.com/pod-product-compliance
Lightning Source LLC
Chambersburg PA
CBHW050102210326
41519CB00015BA/3795